DATE DUE

GAYLORD

PRINTED IN U.S.A.

Comparing
Presidential
Behavior

Recent Titles in
Contributions in Political Science
Series Editor: Bernard K. Johnpoll

Comparing Presidential Behavior

CARTER, REAGAN, AND THE MACHO PRESIDENTIAL STYLE

John Orman

CONTRIBUTIONS IN POLITICAL SCIENCE,
NUMBER 163

Greenwood Press
NEW YORK
WESTPORT, CONNECTICUT
LONDON

Library of Congress Cataloging-in-Publication Data

Orman, John M.
  Comparing presidential behavior.

  (Contributions in political science, ISSN 0147-1066 ;
no. 163)
  Bibliography: p.
  Includes index.
  1. United States—Politics and government—
1977–1981. 2. United States—Politics and government—
1981– . 3. Carter, Jimmy, 1924– . 4. Reagan,
Ronald. 5. Political leadership—United States.
6. Executive advisory bodies—United States. I. Title.
II. Series.
E872.076 1987   353.03'23'0922   86-19445
ISBN 0-313-25516-4 (lib. bdg. : alk. paper)

Library of Congress Catalog Card Number: 86-19445
ISBN: 0-313-25516-4
ISSN: 0147-1066

First published in 1987

Greenwood Press, Inc.
88 Post Road West, Westport, Connecticut 06881

Printed in the United States of America

The paper used in this book complies with the
Permanent Paper Standard issued by the National
Information Standards Organization (Z39.48-1984).

10 9 8 7 6 5 4 3 2 1

COPYRIGHT ACKNOWLEDGMENTS

The author and publisher are grateful to the following for granting the use of
their material:

Parts of Chapter 1 originally appeared in "The Macho Presidential Style," *Indiana Social Studies Quarterly*, XXIX, No. 3 (Winter 1976–1977), pp. 51–60.
Reprinted by permission of Richard Wires.

Parts of Chapter 3 originally appeared in "The President and Interest Group
Access," *Presidential Studies Quarterly* (Fall 1986); parts of Chapter 7 originally
appeared in "Covering the American Presidency, Valenced Reporting in the Periodical Press 1900–1982," *Presidential Studies Quarterly* (Summer 1984). Reprinted by permission of Gordon Hoxie.

Contents

Tables

Acknowledgments

I would like to thank Don Greenberg, chair of the Politics Department at Fairfield University for coauthoring a section on "Reagan and the Launch Syndrome" which appears in chapter 6. We originally presented this to a Northeastern Political Science Association Annual Meeting in New Haven, Connecticut, in 1982.

The following scholars helped me develop my thinking with respect to the macho presidential leadership style: Dorothy Rudoni, Michael Corbett, Fred Meyer, and Ralph Baker of Ball State University; Marjorie Hershey, John Lovell, and Maurice Baxter of Indiana University; Laurellen Porter and John Crittenden of Indiana State University; Thomas Cronin of Colorado College; Bruce Miroff of the State University of New York at Albany; Jeff Fishel of American University; my colleagues at Fairfield University, including Kevin Cassidy, Ed Dew, and Don Greenberg; and Paul Hagner and William Mullen of Washington State University. These scholars cannot be held accountable for the finished product, but they will recognize their influence. Without their interaction over the years, this project could not have been completed.

As always, I want to thank Reenie Demkiw and Natalie and Katie Rose. They gave me the space to finish this book. Sally Williams helped me type some sections of the book and Mildred Vasan and Lisa Reichbach provided the professional guidance from Greenwood Press.

Comparing Presidential Behavior

Introduction

The modern American president arguably holds the most important job in the world. In this nuclear age, the president may be called upon to make the "ultimate decision." He is held accountable by the American public for the state of the economy, and the citizens of the United States look to the president for leadership in both domestic and foreign policy affairs. The president is often called the leader of the "free world" and his actions can influence international politics, trade, and economics. Even rumors about the state of his health can affect the way people behave. In June 1985 rumors that President Ronald Reagan had suffered a heart attack caused the U.S. dollar to drop sharply on the European currency exchanges. It was not until White House spokesman Larry Speakes pronounced that Reagan was "hale and hearty, virile and vigorous, strong and sturdy and fit and feisty,"[1] that the dollar began to climb back to normal levels. Most important, the president of the United States is the quintessential symbol of the country.

Presidential behavior in the 1980s is more complex than presidential behavior in the 1780s. The original Constitution specified only a few roles for the president to play. The president was the chief executive and the commander-in-chief. The Constitution gave the president a diplomatic role with the power to make treaties (by and with the advice and consent of the Senate), and it recognized a legislative role for the president when it gave him veto power. Today, the president plays many more roles; he is to be top economic manager, educator, communicator, world opinion leader, U.S. opinion leader, party leader, and top symbolic leader of the United States. Moreover, for some Americans the president has taken on the role of being the prime target of their hatred, fears, frustrations, and discontent.

The president has to worry about managing foreign and domestic crises in the 1980s and he has to maintain popular support from people, various interest groups, and important opinion leaders. The president has to manage the bureaucracy and must try to implement his policies and decisions in an often unresponsive political environment. If he wants to run for reelection, then the president must play the role of the incumbent "candidate" and must be the power broker for vested capitalist interests in the political system. We ask our president in the 1980s to be a social policy advocate and to make us feel "good" about ourselves.

We offer in exchange for carrying out or attempting to carry out this role behavior some tangible rewards. We offer an annual salary that is less than the average salary that members of the NBA all-star team make, but we provide all the publicity that an individual could ever want. We give the president a nice White House to live in and we provide him with a camp resort, security, airplanes, strategic command jets, helicopters, fine food, a pension, free tickets, entertainment, tennis courts, and a host of other perquisites too numerous to mention.

We offer intangible rewards as well for trying to act out these role demands. We give the incumbent the historic opportunity to be "President of the United States" and we offer him an extraordinary amount of deference. We create a symbol of goodness, greatness, leadership, and competence out of the winner of our election only before we begin to slowly take away this false creation.

As late as December 1980 scholars of the presidency were writing about the "imperiled" state of the presidency. This meant that there were real questions as to whether one person could actually get anything done in the historical context of the 1980s. The presidency was portrayed as an office that did not have the tools to deal with the economic, diplomatic, domestic, and social problems. The United States was described as a nation that could no longer solve its problems, control events in an uncertain world, or control its own destiny. U.S. presidents were portrayed by some observers as being handcuffed by too many restraints that came about in the wake of Vietnam and Watergate.

Within one year, President Reagan had presidential watchers talking about the near-return of the so-called imperial presidency. Reagan had won astounding victories on budget cuts, tax cuts, and spy planes for Saudi Arabia in congressional confrontations. He dropped human rights as the cornerstone of U.S. foreign policy. His administration made a number of decisions to deregulate certain industries, to drop antitrust suits against certain corporations, to open up public lands to the private sector, and to cut back on affirmative action. His administration increased involvement in El Salvador and approved the neutron bomb. Reagan as president unleashed the CIA and the FBI in an effort to return to the environment of the 1950s where the intelligence community had fewer constraints on its behavior. Reagan had almost turned the institution of the presidency around. He rejuvenated the powerless presidency into a presidency that still had much institutional clout because of the leadership abilities of the incumbent. Reagan validated Richard Neustadt's analysis of the presidency, by making maximum use of his bargaining chips and persuasive powers. He narrowed his national agenda and focused attention only on a few items, and he used his ability to communicate effectively and his personal popularity to score a string of impressive victories.

Presidential decisions, choices, and discretion are all influenced by the personality of the incumbent, pragmatic calculations, bureaucratic politics, and the institutional environment of the presidency. Also important are the types of symbols a president selects to manipulate and the types of abilities that the president has as symbol manipulator. Within this complex mix, a president still needs extraordinary timing and luck to be considered a successful president.

THE CARTER PROBLEM

Jimmy Carter is in political exile in Plains, Georgia. It is ironic that one of the great defenders of human rights should be himself a prisoner in his own democracy. He did not break any laws and he was not an unindicted coconspirator in any criminal case. His only "crime" was that he failed to live up to the expectations demanded by the macho presidential style.

Carter's name has become synonymous with a weak, passive, indecisive presidential performance. Candidates for office from his own party do not rush to seek his support. President Ronald Reagan and the Republicans continue to run against "Carter," and Carter left office in January 1981. The media analysts continue to downgrade Carter's presidential performance and he is not respected by presidential watchers and raters of presidential greatness.

Carter was a decent man and a decent president. This fact does not seem to be appreciated. The historical revisionism that upgrades presidential performance in cases like Truman, Eisenhower, and Nixon has not even begun for Carter. It may not begin at all. The memories and accounts of the Carter presidency have been so distorted by media accounts that Carter's name is synonymous with poor presidential performance.

This book will reassess the Carter presidency and the dangerous, so-called macho presidential style which Carter, for not living up to its requirements, was berated by opinion leaders. The book will try to show what the macho presidential style is and why Carter did not live up to it. Moreover, the consequences of not living up to the macho presidential style in a sexist society included poor media coverage of Carter's successes and an incredible press bias against Carter which gave him the most negative press of any twentieth-century president during his time in office. That negative press continues today.

Even after the public has heard from the principals of the Carter administration in the 1980s through books by Carter, Vance, Brzezinski, Jordan, Powell, and Rosalynn Carter, the general impression of the Carter administration is still one of "president malaise." This portrait of Carter as a "do-nothing" president is extremely unfair. This book will show how and why this negative evaluation came about. Moreover, it will demonstrate that this negative evaluation of Carter's presidential performance is inaccurate. Carter certainly was not a "great" president in the sense that presidential raters rank Abraham Lincoln, Franklin D. Roosevelt, and George Washington, but his record in his administration surely compares with John F. Kennedy, Harry S Truman, Woodrow Wilson, and other "near-great" presidents.

It is perhaps time that people stop blaming Carter for the energy crisis, oil embargoes, hostage situations, the Soviet invasion of Afghanistan, recession, high interest rates, and inflation. These were not problems that Carter created, rather they were problems with which his administration had to try to deal. In most cases the problems were beyond his or any president's control.

The Carter administration should be remembered for the Camp David agreements, the energy crisis warnings, the human rights policy in foreign affairs, the lack of CIA secret wars, Carter's sensitivity toward equal rights and justice, the Panama Canal treaty, normalization of relations with the People's Republic of China, the very few soldiers that died in combat during his administration, low deficits, and compassionate social spending. Unfortunately, he is not remembered for these, and it is interesting to discover why this is the case.

THE REAGAN "SUCCESS"

Moreover, this book will try to demonstrate why Ronald Reagan was able to become the "teflon president," as Representative Pat Schroeder dubbed him. Reagan's presidential leadership during his first term will be compared to Carter's exercise of presidential power. Chapter 1 will outline the key presidential myth that keeps the presidential system going, the so-called macho presidential style. The components of the style are examined, and Carter's performance on the continuums of the macho presidential style are compared to Reagan's exercise of macho presidential power. Chapter 2 centers on macho presidents and bureaucratic politics. Carter's advisory activity is examined in this area. In chapter 3, Reagan's advisory activity is outlined and an assessment of the question, "Is Reagan an Active or Passive President?" is considered.

Chapter 4 discusses ways of evaluating macho presidents and chapter 5 evaluates the Carter presidency. In chapter 6, an evaluation of Reagan's first term is offered, and chapter 7 compares periodical coverage of the macho presidential style in the twentieth century. Chapter 7 provides empirical evidence that if Reagan is the teflon president, then Carter certainly is the "velcro" president.

Finally, chapter 8 concludes by reevaluating the macho presidential leadership style and offering an androgynous presidential style for consideration.

NOTE

1. "False Reagan Rumors Send Dollar Plunging," AP story, *Bridgeport Post*, June 14, 1985, p. 39.

1 | The Macho Presidential Style

In one sense the president of the United States is a product that was manufactured by the political system and is the end result of the social and economic systems. The president of the United States holds the highest office in the land and he is recognized as one of the most powerful people in the world. The president serves as a symbol that embodies the fundamental myths of the U.S. political system. The president represents the hope, aspirations, dreams, and successes of the American people, in theory. In short, the president usually represents all that is "good" with the American way of life. Unfortunately, in a sexist political system, the president is also the embodiment of the macho myth.

It should be relatively easy to isolate the key components of the macho presidential style since it is a style of leadership that has remained relatively constant since 1787. Of the thirty-nine different people who have served as president of the United States, all have been men. Each president more or less embodied the seven components of the macho presidential style and the myth of masculinity, as I see it. The presidential macho myth entails that the president be:

1. Competitive in politics and life
2. Sports-minded and athletic
3. Decisive, never wavering or uncertain

4. Unemotional, never revealing true emotions or feelings

5. Strong and aggressive, not weak or passive

6. Powerful

7. A "real man," never "feminine."

All presidents do not fulfill all the demands of the macho myth, but presidents could be placed on a continuum for each of the seven components of the macho myth.

In trying to portray the image of a macho president, men who serve as president must psychologically come to terms with the demands of the macho myth. The macho style of leadership has certain policy consequences in foreign policy and national security arenas, as well as other areas. Presidential behavior can be explained partly by the president's efforts to live up to the macho myth. If a president consistently deviates from the macho myth, he jeopardizes his political power stakes within a sexist system that attempts to define social and political roles by gender. Yet if a president strives to live up to the macho myth to ensure his personal political prestige and his power position, he may find himself in trouble, as this style of leadership can have serious adverse effects on the conduct of public affairs.

The macho myth is not the only myth that governs a president's behavior; there are other myths of the presidency that are also expressed in terms of sexual stereotypes. For example, Thomas Cronin cogently outlined the skeleton of the "textbook presidency" as follows:

1. That the president is the *supreme activist* in the American political system and the *central* figure in the international system as well.

2. That the president is the only American who can be the genuine architect of the U.S. public policy, only *he* can move the country forward.

3. That the president can and should be a *powerful* change agent and should act to *strengthen his* own office and the federal government's rule.

4. That presidents must be the nation's personal and moral leaders, striving always to *attack* problems *frontally* and *aggressively*, interpreting

their *power expansively,* symbolizing the past and future greatness of America and radiating inspirational *confidence.*
5. That only if the *right type of man* is placed in the White House all will be well.[1] [emphasis added]

The problem of asking presidents to live up to the macho myth is the problem of asking someone to be what they are not. The seven components of the macho myth are not inherently male traits nor are they antithetical to femininity. Certainly Gloria Steinem is decisive; women can be unemotional; Billie Jean King is the quintessential "competitive" person; Bella Abzug is a strong and aggressive person; Golda Meir was powerful; women are becoming more sports-minded; and Margaret Thatcher is a "real woman." But the point at hand is that presidents are asked to comply to the seven traits automatically to help perpetuate the myth of masculinity by a sexist political system. The psychic toll can be great since the biological fact of being born with a penis does not determine traits such as decisiveness, unemotionalism, competitiveness, aggressiveness, drive for power, feelings about sports, or the "real" condition of one's sexuality.[2]

A president must be *competitive.* The long struggle through which the president has gone to receive his party's nomination and wage the battle to win the White House attests to the competitive nature of presidential politics. After one wins the top competitive prize within the political system, he is acknowledged for a short time as a competitive superhero during the postelection euphoria. Even Richard Nixon, the constant campaigner, basked in the glory of the winner's circle after his 1968 and 1972 campaign victories. In presidential politics, like professional football, Vince Lombardi's famous dictate applies, "Winning isn't everything. It's the only thing."[3] The macho myth glorifies competition. As Benjamin Bradlee noted about his friend John Kennedy, "He was as competitive as hell."[4] The macho myth requires that the president never "give up" and he must always "fight the good fight." Americans are not kind to quitters, which is probably one reason why Richard Nixon held out so long from his act of resignation. If one quits, he signifies that the competition is over. His "masculinity" is questioned because of the fact that a "*man* would never quit."

Continuing with the macho myth, a president must be *sports-*

minded and *athletic*. This is one of the most fundamental rules of the macho ethic and the one which can cause severe psychological stress on a president who really has no interest in sports or who has no true athletic ability. The organized sports system within the United States is not only an institution that maintains sexism, but sports within the United States is probably the fundamental regime-maintaining institution. When was the last time you heard the National Anthem played not associated with a sporting event? As Thomas Boslooper and Marcia Hayes have noted, "The athlete, for many Americans is still the epitome of patriotism and the masculine ideal."[5]

The macho myth of the presidency requires that the president demonstrate some kind of athletic ability and/or become the nation's number-one sports fan. For example, Teddy Roosevelt was the rugged outdoorsman who "spoke softly and carried a big stick," and Franklin Roosevelt enjoyed sailing, the outdoors, and played some football at Groton before polio curbed some of his participation in sports. Dwight Eisenhower loved football and baseball and admitted, "It would be difficult to overemphasize the importance that I attached to participation in sports."[6] Although John Kennedy injured his back while playing football at Harvard, he remained an avid sports fan. He liked golf, but he treasured the very competitive touch football games among family and staff. In the early 1960s Kennedy made touch football the game of presidents much like Eisenhower made golf the game of presidents during the 1950s. Lyndon Johnson had coached baseball, softball, and basketball, and he knew the power of Texas football. Richard Nixon played some football in college and enjoyed golf. Yet Nixon established the tradition of the president as the nation's top sports fan. Gerald Ford continued this tradition when he became the president as football and golf remained the sports of presidents. The former center for the Michigan football team was suddenly the center of the U.S. political team. Jimmy Carter liked softball, jogging, and tennis.

It was Nixon, however, who revealed a special kind of passion in his love for sports. Nixon especially liked football and he appeared at many of the big games in college and professional sports. One measure of how important a game was could be ascertained if one knew whether or not Nixon phoned *his* congratulations to the champions. The winners were American heros and Nixon liked to be counted among their lot. Former football player Dave Meggysey in his book *Out of Their League*, which exposed the violence, human degradation, racism, drug abuse, and fraud in the all-American game of football, said, "to me it is no accident that Richard Nixon, the most repressive president in American history, is a football freak, and that the sport is rapidly becoming our version of bread and circuses."[7]

It has been no coincidence that women have been systematically excluded from participation within the organized sports system until recent years, since the purpose of the institution has historically been to "produce good men." The "good men"are inducted into a world that emphasizes winning, competition, obedience, decisiveness, strength, authority, loyalty to the team, intense preparation, aggressiveness, power, and "real manhood." The sports world and the political world become one. Women have not always been denied access to the sports world though; their participation and acceptance within sports were at higher levels before World War I.[8] After World War I sport began to take its chauvinistic direction and women began to get channeled into that curious role of "cheerleader."

Presidents often speak in terms of the rhetoric found in the sports world. To throw a long "bomb" for a "score" is to carry out a bombing mission against another country successfully. A whole "new ball game" means that there has been a change in the political environment. "The ball is in their court now," means that the president has shifted responsibility for political action from his desk to another Washingtonian power center. But the most important sports metaphor that presidents like to use is "loyalty to the team." As Woodrow Wilson put it, "If a man will not play in the team, then he does not belong in the team."[9] Kennedy, Johnson, Nixon, Ford, and Carter all called their administrations and staff their "team." The most important bureaucratic virtue has always been "loyalty to the team," and the president acts out his role as coach of the bureaucracy. Janis has outlined some of the consequences of this team loyalty when he observed "that loyalty requires each member to avoid raising controversial issues, questioning weak arguments, or calling a halt to softheaded thinking."[10] Edward Weisband and Thomas Franck's classic work *Resignation in Protest* documents the pressures that are put on members of the team to remain loyal.[11] Presidents like football coaches do not tolerate any "Monday-morning quarterbacking."

The macho myth also requires that presidents be *decisive*, never wavering or uncertain. A president must at least appear to be in control. Decision makers like to believe that they have the power to control events in an uncertain world. Yet the nature of the problems that have confronted post–World War II presidents are not conducive to "decisive" answers. The complex problems require contingencies, options, flexible responses, and pragmatic approaches. These are hardly the conditions that help people to establish their decisiveness. If one appears "fuzzy" or "flip-flops" on an issue, it may say something about the complexity of the issue rather than the lack of a person's manhood.

A president must be in command of the answers at all times, whether or not he has any real faith in them. A president must appear to have the answer to every question that is put to him. A president may answer a question, "I'm sorry I cannot answer your question on the grounds of national security," and get by with that response, but a president cannot answer a question with, "I'm sorry, I don't know the answer to your question," or, "I don't have any solution." This kind of response would attack the macho myth of the presidency. However, during the 1976 and 1980 presidential campaigns, Governor Jerry Brown of California gave some indications that the macho myth was beginning to break. Brown would often say that he did not know all the answers or have all the solutions during his primary campaigns, and later Jimmy Carter would reply at times that he did not have all the answers. If all the answers are not sorted out, it is hard to maintain the macho myth of decisiveness.

A president must be *unemotional*, never revealing true emotions or feelings. As one former occupant of the White House put it, "The great decisions in this office require calm. But I never allow myself to get emotional."[12] Not only is it unmanly, as the macho myth goes, to reveal one's emotions, it is also unpresidential. Witness the classic case of Edmund Muskie during the 1972 New Hampshire presidential primary. Muskie was eliminated as presidential timber by the mass media because he allegedly broke down and cried in public over the "dirty trick" slurs and allegations against his wife. As Warren Farrell has noted, there were no accolades given Muskie or headlines proclaiming "Muskie Not Emotionally Constipated."[13] The *New York Times* instead said that Muskie was "a man who tires easily and tends toward emotional outbursts under pressure."[14]

As national security manager the president must develop a strong sense of what Richard Barnet has termed "bureaucratic machismo."[15] He must be unemotional and, most important, tough. The national security manager develops a curious tolerance for mass homicide and a willingness to use and accept violence as routine. If one is appalled by mass homicide, he is labeled as "irresponsible."[16] As Barnet detailed:

The man who is ready to recommend using violence against foreigners, even when he is overruled, does not damage his reputation for prudence, soundness, or imagination, but the man who recommends putting an issue to the U.N., seeking negotiators, or horrors of horrors, "doing nothing" quickly becomes known as "soft."[17]

Lyndon Johnson had great fears about being the first U.S. president to lose a war; he had an obsession about being tough in the eyes of the world. John Kennedy's great claim to fame, and perhaps his only substantive "great" event in his presidency, was his handling of the Cuban Missile Crisis. The event probably has been covered in academic circles almost as much as Truman's decision to drop the atomic bombs on Japan.[18] The consensus is that Kennedy scored high marks for his "toughness." As one wag put it, "We were eyeball to eyeball with the Russians and they blinked first."

A president must not become emotionally involved in the policy-making process or he will be in contradiction with the macho myth. Presidents are allowed to use the word "compassion for the disadvantaged," or "compassion for senior citizens," but the macho myth does not allow presidents to use the words "love" and "compassion" together. Indeed, in Jimmy Carter's 1976 campaign for the presidency he came under attack for his alleged overuse of the word "love." Near the end of the campaign Carter would often say, "We need more love and compassion, and I am not afraid to say it," or "I'm not ashamed to say it!" Later during his presidency he would drop the emphasis on love and compassion. The macho myth does not allow for love.

A president must be *strong* and *aggressive* according to the macho myth, never weak or passive. Weak and passive presidents never are remembered kindly by the presidential raters and historians.[19] The macho myth demands that presidents talk tough in times when national security threats are perceived. The strong and aggressive president must be ready to engage in the backstage rhetoric and conversations with his intimate advisors which take on the smell of the locker room, as, for example, "I think we better start playin' hard ball," "Let's screw 'em," and the Nixon administration's unique contribution of "ratfucking."[20] A president can never appear to be soft and this applies to near-presidents such as Henry Kissinger. Kissinger even conjured up the old American cowboy myth when he confided to Oriana Fallaci about the reasons for his success:

The Americans love the cowboy, who leads the convoy alone on his horse, the cowboy who comes into town all alone on his horse, and nothing else. Perhaps not even with a gun, because he does not shoot. He acts, and that is enough, being in the right place, at the right time. In sum, a Western. This romantic and surprising character suits me because being alone has always been part of my style, or, if you wish, of my technique.[21]

A president must be *powerful*. In Woodrow Wilson's terminology that means a president must be as big of a man as he can. The literature advocating the strong presidency overwhelmed the discipline of political science in the late 1950s and early 1960s. Richard Neustadt argued that presidents must want to maximize their power. According to Neustadt "Presidents must have a will to power."[22] (This fact must make Friedrich Nietzsche relevant again.) The macho myth requires that the president "lust in his heart" after power. A president who does not wish to maximize his power presumably becomes less of a man.

Finally, the president must be a *real man*, never "feminine." If a president is not decisive, unemotional, competitive, strong and aggressive, powerful, sports-minded and athletic, then by definition he cannot be a real man. Being a real man involves proving one's manhood. The president, presidential candidates, and near-presidents can never be sensitive to gay rights. This would suggest that the president himself might be "queer" or "pansy." When gay activists marched on an Ed Muskie speech in New York in 1972 and demanded that Muskie go on record as supporting a homosexual bill of rights, Muskie became so outraged that he exploded to his staff, "Goddam it, if I've got to be nice to a bunch of sodomites to be elected President, then f____ it."[23] John Lindsay as mayor of New York and as a presidential hopeful had supported such statements for homosexual rights, but Shirley Chisholm was the first presidential candidate to support gay rights during a presidential primary in Massachusetts in April 1972.[24]

A presidential campaign involves a selling process by the two major political parties in which one party says to the other party, in effect, "Our candidate is more of a man than your candidate." Any connection by the president or the presidential candidate to gay people could seriously jeopardize the campaign. That is why Democrats feared that Republicans were going to make a political issue out of the fact that one of Lyndon Johnson's closest political aides, Walter Jenkins, had been arrested in October 1964 in the basement of a Washington YMCA with a homosexual and charged with disorderly conduct.[25] But this controversy did not develop.

Presidents and presidential candidates can have their manhood attacked for many reasons. For some people, George Wallace became "half a man" when he was paralysed from the waist down and confined to a wheelchair after Arthur Bremer's assassination attempt. Jerry Brown was subjected to outrageous allegations about his sexual preferences in *People* magazine and other national media because he did not have any "girlfriends" in 1976 and because he was "uncomfortable" with women. For some people, Gerald Ford really proved his manhood with his handling of the *Mayaguez* incident. Ford proved that he was not going to get kicked around by, in Barry Goldwater's terminology, "some half-assed country."[26] As a youngster Harry Truman refused to go duck hunting on moral grounds, but as Richard Barnet has suggested, he more than made up for his reticence at Hiroshima and Nagasaki.[27] The Nixon team was especially sensitive about the notion of manhood. Kissinger would berate junior members of his staff who had grave reservations about the Cambodian invasion in 1970 and the Christmas bombing of North Vietnam during 1972 by calling them "cowards" and "bleeding hearts."[28] Kissinger even called one colleague a "psychopathic homosexual,"[29] but John Ehrlichman joked that Kissinger himself was "queer."[30] The conservative military man, chief of staff Alexander Haig even carried the gay accusations to the highest level when he joked "that Nixon and Bebe Rebozo had a homosexual relationship, imitating what he called the President's limp-wrist manner."[31] The macho myth of the presidency does not allow for any effeminacy.

The macho presidential style greatly influences presidential behavior. The costs of living by this old myth can be great. If a country requires only one kind of presidential leadership, the macho style, then the incumbent suffers psychologically in trying to live up to the pseudodemands of masculinity. More important, the macho myth limits the wide range of human behavior, possibilities, and potentialities to one rather dull mold. This fashionable and predictable style of presidential leadership forces human beings who happen to be president of the United States into a narrow range of expected and accepted behavior. Both Warren Farrell and Constantina Safilios-Rothschild have outlined, various strategies for liberating males from the psychological oppression that masculinity forces on them.[32] Perhaps we also need strategies to liberate presidents from the macho myth. This would call for a reevaluation of the behavior characteristics that one desires in a president. This book will suggest such a new androgynous style.

CARTER'S FAILURE, REAGAN'S SUCCESS

Part of the failure of the Carter presidency to maintain the macho myth was the fact that Carter allowed his projected image to violate the tenants of the macho presidential style. Although Carter was competitive in politics (he told his staff that he would whip Ted Kennedy's "ass" in the 1980 primaries), he developed the image of being a loser while in the White House. As even Carter has observed about losers, "You show me a good loser and I will show you a loser."[33] Carter tried to be sports minded and athletic by playing tennis, softball, and jogging, but his image as a sports participant was probably best captured when he faltered and collapsed in total exhaustion in the 10 kilometer race over the Catoctin Mountain trail in Maryland in 1979. The picture of the stumbling president made the front pages of news magazines and was circulated internationally. According to Eleanor Clift and Thomas DeFrank, Carter thought the trail was too steep and that he was not capable of completing the race. His jogging partner and personal physician, Dr. William Lukash, egged Carter on until Carter agreed to compete in the meet cosponsored by Lukash's running club.[34] Carter gave in to the macho pressures with disastrous results.

The many shifts in the Carter policies gave the impression that Carter was indecisive and uncertain. For example, Carter first argued that unemployment was the number-one problem for his economic policy and then he abruptly switched to ordering inflation as his top priority. Carter waffled on U.N. votes often, and he switched positions on the question of deregulation of natural gas.

Carter often gave the appearance of being too emotional for a macho presidency. He cried in public on occasions when he was extremely happy or when he attended funerals. He also talked of love and compassion as he pushed a human rights foreign policy in his early international rhetoric.

Carter did not appear as a strong or aggressive president. He kept the United States out of military involvement in Angola, Iran during the revolution, and Nicaragua, for example. He was perceived by some as a president who let the Soviets push him around and as a president who allowed militant terrorists to embarrass the United States in Teheran. Carter was not perceived as a particularly powerful president either. He was cited for his inability to "control" Congress and the bureaucracy. His efforts to "de-imperialize" the presidency were interpreted by some as a total abandonment of the so-called strong presidency.

Finally, Carter did not project the image of being a "real man." He was reported to have been sensitive about his physical stature, which was recorded at five feet, nine and one-half inches. Though this is about average height for American males, this made Carter among the shortest of American presidents. Moreover, Carter considered the advice of his wife, Rosalynn Carter, when making many important decisions. Some observers criticized the new liberated role that Rosalynn Carter was establishing for First Ladies, that is, of policy advisor to the president.

These efforts by Carter, which went against the stereotype of the macho presidential style, were quite refreshing in my judgment, because the consequences of the macho style can be devastating in terms of foreign and domestic policies. In short, Carter was a *person*. He showed a wide range of emotions, he considered his wife to be an equal partner in their marriage, he was no prisoner to ideology, and he was singularly impressive as a man of peace. Rather than being rewarded for these qualities by commentators, presidential watchers, and the American public, Carter was widely attacked by many for failing to live up to the demands of the macho presidential style.

Ronald Reagan has no such problems. Reagan is the quintessential macho president. Moreover, he appears to be the most adept president since Franklin D. Roosevelt at manipulating political symbols. Reagan brought many prepackaged images with him to the presidency. He was the small-town boy and the former movie star. He was the Barry Goldwater conservative and the former pragmatic Governor of California.[35] He was the former president of a labor union (the Screen Actors Guild) and he was the millionaire rancher.[36] He was the last great hope for the conservative Right and he was the constant banquet speaker. He was ever the campaigner and he was the extraordinary speechmaker. He was the aging, affable politician in the body of an energetic younger man. Although Reagan was never like Carter in 1976 who was all things to all people with respect to image, Reagan still provided a wide array of symbolic baggage for the electorate. Most important, Reagan personified the macho presidential style.

Reagan was very competitive in politics and life. He had come extremely close to defeating an incumbent President Gerald Ford from his own party in a 1976 Republican nomination bid. Rather than being labeled as a loser, Reagan scored points for his incredible showing and for reuniting the party behind Gerald Ford. In the 1980 election he clearly became a winner's winner by knocking off his Republican opposition early on the primary trail. Finally, he proved that he was the ultimate winner by defeating Jimmy Carter in an electoral college landslide which the experts had not been able to predict.

Reagan was sportsminded and athletic. He rode horses and worked the ranch.[37] He was an all-American cowboy and he had even played George Gipp, "the Gipper," in the Knute Rockne movie. Reagan had cowboy hats and cowboy boots. His wife, Nancy, even owned a gun. Moreover, Reagan wore real cowboy jeans when he worked and played on the ranch.

Reagan appeared very decisive. When he made a decision, he did not waver, waffle, or appear uncertain. Reagan had been giving essentially the same stock speech about government during the 1960s and 1970s so it was easy for him to appear consistent. His rhetoric was easily identified and his position with respect to basic issues did not appear to be subject to change.

Reagan, however, could not be characterized as completely unemotional. Although he always appeared in control of himself, he had the ability in his stock speeches to get choked up with emotion and to allow his voice to falter at the right places, usually at the invocation of the name of "God."[38] He projected an excellent sense of humor and he looked as though he was incapable of raging against his staff or loved ones in anger.[39]

In his rhetoric, Reagan was the "cold warrior" who could still think in terms of monolithic Communist expansion.[40] He condemned those who could be "soft" on Communists and he denounced appeasement in any form. Reagan appeared to project the image of a strong, aggressive, and powerful leader. He talked tough to the Soviets and the Cubans. He made it clear that he wanted the CIA to be able to protect American interests whenever the president called upon it to do so. He talked about the need to make the American military strong again, as if it were weak in the 1980s. He would negotiate only through strength and by letting the "enemy" know that it had something to fear. He adopted Richard Nixon's advice to presidents for a return to the "strong presidency." He selected former General Alexander Haig to be his secretary of state and he wanted the shackles taken off of the intelligence agencies. He made it clear that the United States would not make "human rights" the cornerstone of the Reagan foreign policy, rather the struggle to fight international terrorism would be the central focus. Moreover, Reagan declared that it was better to side with an authoritarian dictator in the Third World who committed human rights violations and was friendly to the United States than to allow a friendly dictator to be overthrown by Communists who were unfriendly to U.S. interests.[41]

Finally, Reagan was a real man. He still looked virile and he still looked like a movie star. He was a celebrity who surrounded himself with famous people and who had famous friends. He had an attractive wife, a former movie actress, who loved him very much. His wife appeared to be the supportive political wife who would never upstage her husband or try to become a policy advisor to her husband.[42] Reagan looked attractive in formal attire and clearly gave the impression that he was in command of his relationships, his presidency, and his country at all times.

By scoring high marks on each of the seven baselines for the macho presidential style, Reagan was able to reinstitute the chief symbol of the presidency. Earlier I warned of the serious consequences of this continued style of presidential leadership because it limited the possibilities of presidential behavior and because it forced incumbents to behave in certain self-destructive patterns of macho behavior. The Reagan administration should provide another test of the consequences of the macho presidential style.

Most important, Reagan believed the presidency to have an important educational function. Reagan enjoyed speaking to the nation directly and playing the role of wise teacher and comforter. He clearly liked the role as chief communicator within the Reagan administration since he clearly was the best political communicator and symbolic manipulator to come to the presidency in about forty years. Once again, the question faced the Reagan administration, "At what point does an administration have to provide tangible successes to support symbolic images?" For Reagan the answer was, clearly, immediately.

NOTES

1. Thomas Cronin, *The State of the Presidency*, 2d ed. (Boston: Little, Brown, 1980), pp. 75-118.

2. Judith Hole and Ellen Levine, "The Politics of Biological Differences," *Rebirth of Feminism*, (New York: Quadrangle, 1971), pp. 192-93.

3. Quoted in Thomas Boslooper and Marcia Hayes, *The Femininity Game* (New York: Stein & Day, 1973), p. 101.

4. Benjamin Bradlee, *Conversations with Kennedy* (New York: Pocket Books, 1976), p. 207.

5. Boslooper and Hayes, *The Femininity Game*, p. 97.

6. Dwight Eisenhower, *At Ease* (New York: Avon Books, 1968), p. 16.

7. Dave Meggysey, *Out of Their League* (New York: Paperback Library, 1971), p. 8.

8. Boslooper and Hayes, *The Femininity Game*, pp. 92-96.

9. Aileen Kraditor, *The Ideas of the Woman Suffrage Movement, 1890-1920* (Garden City, N.Y.: Anchor, 1971), p. 193.

10. Irving Janis, *Victims of Groupthink* (Boston: Houghton Mifflin, 1972), p. 12.

11. Edward Weisband and Thomas Franck, *Resignation in Protest* (New York: Penguin, 1976).

12. Richard Nixon, quoted in Bruce Mazlish, *In Search of Nixon* (Baltimore: Pelican Books, 1973), p. xx.

13. Warren Farrell, *The Liberated Man* (New York: Random House, 1974), p. 69.

14. "New Hampshire Presidential Primary," editorial, *New York Times*, March 9, 1972, p. 32.

15. Richard Barnet, *Roots of War* (Baltimore: Pelican, 1973), p. 109.

16. Ibid.

17. Ibid.

18. See Graham Allison, *Essence of Decision* (Boston: Little, Brown, 1971); E. Abel, *The Missile Crisis* (New York: Bantam Books, 1966); Irving Janis, *Victims of Groupthink*; Robert F. Kennedy, *Thirteen Days* (New York: Norton, 1969); and Roger Hilsman, *To Move a Nation* (New York: Doubleday, 1967).

19. See the Schlesinger polls of 1948 and 1962; Clinton Rossiter, *The American Presidency*, rev. ed. (New York: New American Library, 1960); and James Barber, *The Presidential Character* (Englewood Cliffs, N.J.: Prentice-Hall, 1972 and 1977).

20. See Gerald Gold, ed. *White House Transcripts* (New York: Bantam Books, 1974).

21. Boslooper and Hayes, *The Femininity Game*, p. 97.

22. Richard Neustadt, quoted in Peter Sperlich, "Bargaining and Overload: An Essay on Presidential Power," in A. Wildavsky, *The Presidency* (Boston: Little, Brown, 1969), p. 171.

23. Theodore White, *The Making of the President 1972* (New York: Atheneum, 1973), p. 76.

24. Shirley Chisholm, *The Good Fight* (New York: Harper & Row, 1973), p. 82.

25. Arthur Schlesinger, Jr., *The Coming to Power* (New York: Chelsea and McGraw-Hill, 1971).

26. Bill Moyers, "Image," *Newsweek*, June 2, 1975, p. 80.

27. Richard Barnet, *Roots of War*, p. 17.

28. Bob Woodward and Carl Bernstein, *The Final Days* (New York: Simon & Schuster, 1976), p. 192; and see Marvin Kalb and Bernard Kalb, *Kissinger* (New York: Dell, 1975), p. 196.

29. Woodward and Bernstein, *The Final Days*, p. 189.
30. Ibid., p. 187.
31. Ibid., p. 197.
32. See Warren Farrell, *The Liberated Male* (New York: Random House, 1974), and Constantina Safilios-Rothschild, *Women and Social Policy* (Englewood Cliffs, N.J.: Prentice-Hall, 1974), pp. 72-95.
33. Robert Turner, *I'll Never Lie to You: Jimmy Carter in His Words* (New York: Ballantine Books, 1976), p. 7.
34. Eleanor Clift and Thomas DeFrank, "Tales of the Carter Years," *Newsweek*, January 19, 1981, p. 27.
35. Robert Lindsey, "What the Record Says about Reagan," *New York Times Magazine*, June 29, 1980, pp. 12-20ff.
36. Peter Goldman, "Reagan up Close," *Newsweek*, July 21, 1980, pp. 25-53.
37. Roger Rosenblatt, "Man of the Year: Out of the Past, Fresh Choices for the Future," *Time*, January 5, 1981, pp. 11-37.
38. Reagan liked to mention the word "God" in his speeches. During his acceptance speech at the 1980 Republican National Convention, Reagan saved his emotional reference to God until the end of his speech. During his inaugural address on January 20, 1981, Reagan appeared to be moved by his reference to God. As Reagan told interviewer Laurence Barrett, "This is a nation under God. It is still on our coins: 'In God we trust.' " See "An Interview with Ronald Reagan," *Time*, January 5, 1981, p. 32.
39. Reagan could tell jokes about himself and he easily carried on the banter between himself and friends like Jimmy Stewart, Johnny Carson, and Frank Sinatra. His comedic delivery style was fully developed over the years as a banquet speaker and Reagan put this to good use in interviews, press conferences, and live addresses to the nation.
40. See Hedrick Smith, "Reagan: What Kind of World Leader?" *New York Times Magazine*, November 16, 1980, pp. 47ff.
41. See Richard Nixon, *The Real War* (New York: Warner Books, 1980), p. 250, and see Nixon's advice to those who would negotiate with the Soviets, pp. 293-95.
42. Nancy Reagan returned the role of First Lady to the quiescent supporter after Rosalynn Carter had dramatically expanded the role. If Rosalynn Carter democratized the role and became a liberated populist, then Nancy Reagan reinstated the First Lady as fashion queen, elitist, and party giver.

2 | Macho Presidents and Bureaucratic Politics

After a macho presidential candidate has been elected, Americans ask their president to be decisive and unemotional. Americans generally like a president who makes decisions, who takes control of a situation, and who provides leadership by telling others how to deal with problems. Americans do like some amount of flexibility and pragmatism in their chief executive, yet they do not like the elected head of state to be indecisive. Moreover, a president is not respected by presidential watchers, opinion leaders, fellow Washingtonians, and the public when he loses control of his emotions. We ask the president to suspend his humanity, never to reveal his true emotional state or feelings, and to act like he is not touched by the full range of human emotional experience. The president can show joy, but not too much. He can show fear, but not too much. The president can show anger, but not too much. He can show emotional hurt, but not too much. The president should not cry in public. He should display all the emotional feeling that the head of a large multinational corporation would display. In short, the president of the United States is asked to provide the manly image of being in control of his emotions at all times. This emotional constipation can be very costly to the country as it props up the image of the macho presidential style.

The American president is involved in a game played out usually in the bureaucracy with and between mostly other men. The game pits intellectual toughness, hardball politics, and the bureaucratic machismo of the players who want to impress the president and to help him make decisions. Sometimes the players even try to make the decisions for the president with the hope that he will ratify and approve of their choices. All players of the bureaucratic politics game must appear decisive and in control of their emotions so that the president can appear decisive and in control of his emotions.

A macho president who wants to appear decisive and to appear in control of his emotions has the ability to get support from staff and advisors by demanding loyalty to the "team."

How is this bureaucratic politics game played out? Graham Allison and Morton Halperin are two proponents of the bureaucratic politics paradigm and they provide an understanding as to just how the game is played.

According to their analysis, government leaders have competitive interests rather than homogeneous ones. Therefore, one must look at: (a) Who plays? (That is, whose interests and behavior have an important effect on the government's decisions and actions? Are they senior players or junior players?), and (b) What determines each player's stand? (What determines his perceptions and interests which lead to a stand? Are they national security interests, organizational interests, domestic interests, or personal interests?)[1]

For Halperin and Allison, the action channels structure the policy games by preselecting the major players and by determining the usual points of entrance into the bureaucratic politics game. They observed:

Bargaining advantages stem from control of implementation, control over information that enables one to define the problem and identify the available options, persuasiveness with other players (including players outside the bureaucracy) and the ability to affect other players' objectives in other, including domestic political games.[2]

This bureaucratic politics game is played out by elite males with the president acting as a key player. At times the president is able to control the direction of the game because he has the ability, especially in national security policy making, to manipulate other macho men by using the trump cards of presidential loyalty and control of the excessive presidential secrecy system.

PRESIDENTIAL LOYALTY TO LOYALTY

Philosopher Josiah Royce propounded a philosophy called the philosophy of loyalty.[3] It is a philosophy adopted by American presidents. Presidential demands for staff loyalty usually fall into four distinct categories: loyalty to the president, loyalty to the presidency, loyalty to the team, and loyalty to national security. All the demands ask a staff member or worker to be loyal both to a cause and to the cause of loyalty.

Loyalty to loyalty within the modern presidency has caused some interesting policy-making malfunctions. In the 1940s, it became extremely difficult for policymakers and scientists who might have had second thoughts about the production of the atomic bomb in the Manhattan Project to express these ideas because of their loyalty to loyalty. When some members of the project became aware of the awesome destructive capabilities of the bomb, there was no massive resignation of scientists and workers to protest the new escalation of potential violence. After Harry S Truman came to the White House upon the death of Franklin D. Roosevelt in 1945, Truman first became aware of the atomic bomb. Once this costly project had developed its own bureaucratic momentum under the Roosevelt administration, it left Truman no choice but to continue the program. Much has been written about the Truman decision to drop the bomb, but most of the literature fails to concentrate on the "groupthink" aspects of the decision, to use Irving Janis's terminology. Truman's loyalty to loyalty and the demands that were placed on staff, advisors, and scientists distorted information channels. One consequence of this loyalty-to-loyalty mentality was that the decision to build the bomb quickly became the decision to drop the bombs, since Nagasaki was devastated shortly after Hiroshima.

In World War II, the pressures from loyalty to loyalty also created the climate where the relocation of American citizens to concentration centers by presidential fiat was allowed to take place. The internment of Japanese-Americans and the denial of their civil liberties, civil rights, and property rights was carried out in this country with virtually no dissent, because Roosevelt was able to create a situation that asked other Americans to be loyal to loyalty.

Another consequence of the presidential loyalty-to-loyalty mentality came in the late 1940s and early 1950s in the form of loyalty programs. The loyalty programs were instruments that allowed presidents to secure their secrets more efficiently within the secrecy system. If workers could be released on the basis that they *might* pose a security threat, then the system of presidential secrecy could be maintained. The probability that secret information would leak out was presumably reduced under the presidential loyalty programs, but this did not necessarily provide constitutional justifications for such programs.

Truman's loyalty program was established in 1947 by executive order directing the Federal Bureau of Investigation to investigate all federal employees and to forward charges of disloyalty to loyalty review boards within the various bureaus. Hearings were conducted to determine whether accused workers were in fact disloyal, but the accused had no right to examine the FBI files or to learn the name of their accusers.[4] If an individual belonged or had belonged to any organizations that the attorney general labeled "subversive,"[5] the loyalty review boards considered this fact evidence of disloyalty. By 1953 the attorney general labeled over 200 organizations as subversive, and the loyalty review boards no longer had to prove disloyalty for discharge; they could remove employees if they could find "reasonable doubt" of the employee's loyalty.[6] Dwight Eisenhower established a wider security program by executive order in 1953 which expanded the disloyalty criteria to include "sexual immorality, perversion, drug addiction, conspiracy, sabotage, treason, unauthorized disclosure of classified information, and refusal to testify before authorized government bodies on the grounds of possible self-incrimination."[7] Not only could presidents demand loyalty but they could also define in terms of personal orientation the kind of person they wanted to work in government.

In the 1950s and 1960s presidential loyalty to loyalty also played an important part in creating a climate where groupthink could occur. This social-psychological phenomena occurs in presidential decision making, according to Irving Janis, when advisors share an illusion of invulnerability, engage in collective efforts to rationalize, have a sense of inherent morality, stereotype the enemy, pressure dissenters, use self-censorship and mind guards, believe in a shared illusion of unanimity, and protect the group from adverse information in the decision-making process.[8] Janis outlines two U.S. foreign policy fiascoes, the Bay of Pigs invasion and the decision to escalate the war in Vietnam, as examples of groupthink's influence on the decision-making process. Loyalty to loyalty also made it difficult for reasonable advisors to challenge presidents and it allowed administration participants to engage and order secret bombings, free-fire zones, deployment of antipersonnel mines, defoliation, and napalming in Indochina.

With respect to the intelligence community, the notion of loyalty to loyalty allowed intelligence agents and operatives in the CIA to engage in domestic surveillance of American citizens, to participate in assassination plots against foreign heads of state, to test hallucinogenic drugs on unwitting Americans, to open first-class letters sent by citizens, to overthrow governments in other countries, and to engage in secret ground wars.[9] Loyalty to loyalty in the FBI allowed agents to engage in illegal domestic wiretapping, to act as agent provocateurs and infiltrate various groups, to harass Martin Luther King, Jr., by trying to destroy his marriage and ability to lead the civil rights movement, and to engage in illegal break-ins among a host of other questionable activities. Agents were simply following orders and remaining loyal to the idea of loyalty to the president, or the presidency, or to the team, or to "national security."[10]

In the 1970s, the revelations that came out during the Watergate years indicated that the power of loyalty to loyalty allowed members of the Nixon administration routinely to break the law in order to engage in the Watergate cover-up. Young men, particularly Jeb Stuart Magruder in *An American Life* and John Dean in *Blind Ambition*, told stories of how they blindly followed the line of the Nixon administration and broke the law.[11]

Loyalty to loyalty distorts the decision-making process by protecting the president from criticism and dissent. It corrupts the decision-making process by creating a climate that does not allow for critical and ethical thinking on the part of public servants. The loyalty-to-loyalty philosophy does not provide a clear framework for the use of moral reasoning and for making free choices. The public servant is absolved of the consequences of his actions by blaming presidents for giving the orders.

The organization of the presidency clearly needs some central organizing principle other than loyalty to loyalty. Presidents need advice systems that do not equate criticism and dissent of policies with disloyalty. Perhaps presidents should establish a policy of rejecting those servants who are loyal to the idea of loyalty and so promoting those servants who are disloyal to the idea of loyalty to loyalty.

ADVISORY ACTIVITY IN THE CARTER ADMINISTRATION

There are many ways that presidential advisors can communicate their positions on issues to the president of the United States in the policy-making process. Advisors can send memoranda to the president, telephone the president, send out "trail balloon" leaks in the media, meet informally with the president, and interact with the president in the formal fundamental bureaucratic policy-making device—the scheduled meeting. While all of these were probably important methods of communication with the president for advisors in the Carter administration, the only method of interaction that can be examined empirically is the formal scheduled meetings of the Carter administration. This section will examine the advisory activity of the Carter administrators as measured by formal scheduled meetings with the president.

Whether the Carter administration provided an open presidency after the Watergate years is still a debatable proposition. However, one fact is not in doubt. The records of the Carter administration as provided in the weekly releases of the *Public Papers of the Presidents* show for the first time a detailed account of the scheduled meetings that Carter had each day. By examining which advisors the president met with over time, one can monitor White House advisory activity.

Methods

In order to measure interactions with President Carter in the formal meeting setting from the *Public Papers of the Presidents* a process was devised to count each interaction. For example, if a meeting was listed as "March 8, 1977, the President met with Dr. Arthur Burns, Chairman of the Board of Governors of the Federal

Reserve System, and Vice-President Mondale," the meeting would count as one interaction with Dr. Burns and one interaction with Walter Mondale. Thus two interactions were recorded even though only one meeting took place. The president had numerous meetings where there were multiple participants and he had many meetings where only one person attended.

Problems

This method of measuring access to the president by the Carter advisors in the formal setting of a meeting does not measure influence. There are no recordings of the meetings by tape or by minutes, so one is not in a position to chart what kind of advice was given or indeed what policy area was discussed. Thus, a five-minute formal meeting with Hamilton Jordan to discuss the White House tennis court schedules would count the same as a two-hour briefing from David Aaron on national security matters. Both Jordan and Aaron would receive a score of one for the meeting with the president. In meetings where there were many participants, one cannot measure who did most of the talking and who remained relatively silent on the issue. Each participant in the meeting would receive the same score.

Moreover, this method combines meetings on policy making with meetings on implementation, evaluation, information exchanges, and political strategy meetings. A meeting with the president for whatever purpose, as long as it was listed as an official meeting, is counted. Thus purposes and intents of meetings become confused.

Despite these problems, the fact that the Carter administration decided to publish the schedules of the president's weekly meetings allows one to measure empirically who was seeing the president and how frequently certain advisors were getting to the top. Access to the president can be empirically verified.

Participants in Carter Administration Meetings

Aaron, David L., Deputy Assistant for National Security Affairs.

Adams, Brock, Secretary of Transportation, 1977-79.

Andrus, Cecil, Secretary of Interior.

Bell, Griffin, Attorney General, 1977-79.

Bergland, Bob, Secretary of Agriculture.

Blumenthal, W. Michael, Secretary of the Treasury, 1977-79.

Bosworth, Barry, Director of Wage and Price Stability.

Brown, Harold, Secretary of Defense.

Brzezinski, Zbigniew, Assistant to the President for National Security Affairs.

Burger, Warren, Chief Justice of the Supreme Court.

Burns, Arthur, Chairman of the Federal Reserve Board, 1977-78.

Califano, Joseph, Secretary of Health, Education and Welfare 1977-79.

Carter, Rosalynn, wife of the president.

Civiletti, Benjamin, Attorney General, 1979-81.

Costle, Douglas M., Administrator of Environmental Protection Agency.

Cutler, Lloyd N., Counsel to the President, 1979-81.

Donovan, Hedley, W., Senior Advisor to the President, 1979-81.

Duncan, Charles, Secretary of Energy, 1980-81.

Eizenstat, Stuart E., Assistant to the President for Domestic Affairs and Policy.

Goldschmidt, Neil, Secretary of Transportation, 1979-81.

Harris, Patricia R., Secretary of Housing and Urban Development 1977-79, and Secretary of Health, Education, and Welfare later Health and Human Services, 1979-81.

Hufstedler, Shirley, Secretary of Education, 1979-81.

Hyland, William G., Senior staff member of the National Security Council.

Jordan, Hamilton, Chief of Staff.

Kahn, Alfred E., Advisor to the President on Inflation and Chairman on Wage and Price Stability.

Klutznick, Philip, Secretary of Commerce, 1979-81.

Kreps, Juanita, Secretary of Commerce, 1977-79.

Lance, Bert, Director of Office of Management and Budget, 1977.

Landrieu, Moon, Secretary of Housing and Urban Development, 1979-81.

Marshall, Ray, Secretary of Labor.

McDonald, Alonzo L., Assistant to the President.

McHenry, Donald, Ambassador to the United Nations, 1979-81.

McIntyre, James T., Director of Office of Management and Budget, 1977-81.

Miller, G. William, Chairman of Federal Reserve Board, 1978-79, and Secretary of Treasury, 1979-81.

Mondale, Walter, Vice President.

Moore, Frank, Assistant to the President for Congressional Liaison.

Muskie, Edmund, Secretary of State, 1980-81.

Powell, Jody, Press Secretary.

Press, Frank, Director of Office of Science and Technology Policy.

Schlesinger, James R., Secretary of Energy, 1977-78.

Schultze, Charles, Chairman of Council of Economic Advisors.

Turner, Stansfield, Director of the Central Intelligence Agency.

Vance, Cyrus, Secretary of State, 1977-80.

Volcker, Paul, Chairman of the Federal Reserve Board, 1979-81.

Webster, William, Director of the Federal Bureau of Investigation.

Wexler, Anne, Assistant to the President.

Young, Andrew, Ambassador to the United Nations, 1977-79.

Results

Table 2.1 provides a breakdown of the number of meetings or interactions with President Carter from the national security and foreign policy advisors from 1977 to 1981. Clearly, the president's advisor for national security, Zbigniew Brzezinski, emerges as the dominant advisor. Brzezinski tallied many meetings with the president because of his early morning briefings, but Brzezinski was much more active than this. He appeared at meetings with Secretary of State Cyrus Vance, in meetings with CIA Director Stansfield Turner, in meetings with Secretary of Defense Harold Brown, and in meetings with Hamilton Jordan. Brzezinski's presence was pervasive in the national security and foreign policy arena: he made up over 64 percent of all interactions in this policy area. Vance has recently complained, on the talk-show circuit to promote his book, about the fact that he "felt" shut out from the president.[12] Table

Table 2.1
National Security and Foreign Policy Advice, Carter Presidency,
1977–81

Name	Meetings(per year, first half and second half) 1977 (1st)(2nd)		1978 (1st)(2nd)		1979 (1st)(2nd)		1980-81 (1st)(2nd)		Total
Brzezinski	157	161	128	123	126	116	140	110	1061
Aaron	2	12	11	14	7	7	13	8	74
NSC	4	1	1	1	0	2	2	1	12
Hyland	0	4	0	0	0	0	0	0	4
Joint Chiefs	0	3	1	1	2	0	0	0	7
Generals	0	2	2	1	0	0	0	0	5
Turner	30	23	20	17	21	7	10	3	131
Brown	15	22	17	24	19	18	26	20	161
Vance	15	30	23	36	20	18	13	-	155
Muskie	-	-	-	-	-	-	13	19	32
Young	4	1	2	2	1	1	-	-	11
McHenry	-	-	-	-	-	1	1	0	2
Totals	227	259	205	219	196	170	218	161	1655

2.1 indicates that Vance had a right to feel cut off from the president. Vance provided only 9.3 percent of the total interactions in this combined policy area.

The National Security Council met only twelve times during this period and it was not a central vehicle to provide the president with national security advice. Brzezinski and David Aaron, deputy assistant for national security affairs, provided more than enough national security advice. Turner's access to the president diminished over time as Turner met with the president fifty three times in the first year of the administration and only thirteen times in the last year of the administration.

Table 2.2 shows the pattern of access by staff advisors for the

Table 2.2
Staff Advice, Carter Presidency, 1977–81

Name	Meetings(per year, first half and second half)								
	1977		1978		1979		1980-81		
	(1st)	(2nd)	(1st)	(2nd)	(1st)	(2nd)	(1st)	(2nd)	Total
Mondale	60	95	46	53	64	44	41	19	422
Staff	22	16	1	1	0	0	0	1	41
Cabinet	21	18	13	9	7	2	3	2	75
Powell	0	0	0	0	0	0	0	1	1
Jordan	1	0	31	37	35	18	26	0	148
Watson	2	3	1	0	2	6	4	16	34
Eizenstat	4	10	5	2	18	14	12	4	69
Moore	6	5	66	42	79	75	88	57	418
R. Carter	5	27	22	14	14	8	8	2	100
Wexler	-	-	-	-	2	2	0	1	5
McDonald	-	-	-	-	-	4	8	3	15
Cutler	-	-	-	-	-	6	17	9	32
Donovan	-	-	-	-	-	20	29	3	52
Totals	121	174	185	158	221	199	236	118	1412

Carter administration from 1977 to 1981. Vice-President Walter Mondale emerged as the person who had the most meetings with the president. This confirms the speculation that the Carter-Mondale relationship was a radical transformation in the relationship of the vice-president to the president. Mondale was not a "do-nothing" vice president and in fact he often attended meetings with the president. Though comparative data is not availble for previous administrations, it is difficult to believe that vice-presidents like Hubert Humphrey or Spiro Agnew had as much access to their presidents as Mondale did to his.

In the first year, Carter relied on the organized staff meeting as a tool for interaction, but this quickly ceased. After thirty eight staff meetings in 1977, the numbers fell off to two meetings in 1978, no meetings in 1979, and one meeting in the last year. Cabinet meetings also declined over time but not at the same rate as staff meetings.

As the president's chief domestic policy advisor, Stuart Eizenstat did not meet with the president very often in formal meetings. Moreover, Hamilton Jordan, a key advisor by most accounts, did not meet with the president as much as one would have thought in formal settings. Clearly, Jody Powell, the president's press secretary had to be meeting with the president informally because Powell only logged one official meeting with Carter.

Finally, the most significant fact in Table 2.2 is that Rosalynn Carter emerged as an important policy advisor to the president. She met with the president one hundred times in official scheduled meetings presumably to talk about politics and some family matters. Informally, of course, she had the greatest access to the president but officially and formally she also was considered a policy advisor.[13]

The Carter administration brought forth a remarkable and radical change in the relationship between presidents of the United States and their spouses in terms of policy. In the past, the so-called First Lady was outspoken on a very few political issues, as was Betty Ford, or she had a few "pet projects" as did Eleanor Roosevelt or Lady Bird Johnson or even Jacqueline Kennedy. Other than a few very minor policy situations, presidential spouses had virtually no policy impact. Indeed, their very role and existence was to have *no* policy impact. Their role was to be supportive, passive, helpful, and uninvolved. They were the president's adornment and were in no way considered to be capable of operating in the president's policy domain. When Harry Truman always said he would have to ask the "Boss" (meaning Bess Truman) if he could do something, he was being humorous. The model First Lady is a smiling woman like Pat Nixon or Nancy Reagan. Besides Mrs. Woodrow Wilson, who kept the White House running while her husband was recovering from a stroke, every past First Lady has been inconsequential to presidential policy. This was not the case for Rosalynn Carter. She was indeed a policy advisor.

Table 2.3 charts the advice activity for the Carter presidency

Table 2.3
Economic Advice, Carter Presidency, 1977–81

Name	Meetings(per year, first half and second half) 1977 (1st)	(2nd)	1978 (1st)	(2nd)	1979 (1st)	(2nd)	1980-81 (1st)	(2nd)	Total
Blumenthal	15	22	9	6	16	3	-	-	71
Miller	-	-	3	4	1	6	6	4	24
Burns	4	5	2	-	-	-	-	-	11
Volcker	-	-	-	-	-	2	2	1	5
Schultze	26	30	17	18	23	14	18	3	149
Kreps	4	6	1	1	2	2	-	-	16
Klutznick	-	-	-	-	-	-	4	0	4
Lance	37	15	-	-	-	-	-	-	52
McIntyre	-	16	19	16	30	29	19	9	138
Kahn	-	-	-	3	14	9	10	3	39
Bosworth	-	-	-	1	11	-	-	-	12
Totals	86	94	51	49	97	65	59	20	521

from 1977 to 1981 in terms of economic advice. Charles Schultze, the head of the Council of Economic Advisors, was naturally the principal economic advisor. Yet compared to other kinds of advice, there were not too many meetings that centered on economic matters. Even during times of high inflation in the Carter era, the president did not meet very often face-to-face with his inflation fighters, as witnessed by few meetings with Alfred Kahn and Barry Bosworth. Carter had a few face-to-face meetings with the chairman of the Federal Reserve Board, Paul Volcker, no doubt to plead that interest rates should be lowered. Table 2.3 also reveals some budgetary activity with meetings from the heads of the OMB, Bert Lance and then James T. McIntyre.

Table 2.4 indicates the advice activity from domestic policy ad-

Table 2.4
Domestic Policy/Cabinet Level Advice, Carter Presidency, 1977–81

Name	Meetings(per year, first half and second half)								
	1977		1978		1979		1980-81		
	(1st)	(2nd)	(1st)	(2nd)	(1st)	(2nd)	(1st)	(2nd)	Total
Webster	0	0	0	0	0	0	0	1	1
Bell	2	11	4	0	2	-	-	-	19
Civiletti	-	-	-	-	-	1	0	1	2
Burger	0	1	0	0	0	0	0	0	1
Costle	0	0	0	1	1	0	0	2	4
Califano	7	9	6	1	3	1	-	-	27
Harris	0	4	3	0	0	7	2	0	16
Landrieu	-	-	-	-	-	5	3	0	8
Schlesinger	9	8	5	1	8	2	-	-	33
Duncan	-	-	-	-	-	3	3	0	6
Marshall	6	10	10	2	1	4	5	0	38
Bergland	4	5	2	0	0	4	5	1	21
Andrus	2	4	3	1	0	3	2	1	16
Adams	7	5	0	4	2	1	-	-	19
Goldschmidt	-	-	-	-	-	5	6	0	11
Hufstedler	-	-	-	-	-	-	2	0	2
Press	0	0	0	2	1	0	0	1	4
Totals	37	57	33	12	18	36	28	7	228

visors in cabinet-level positions in the Carter presidency from 1977 to 1981. What is most remarkable about the pattern shown in Table 2.4 is the lack of activity in various domestic policy areas as measured by the number of interactions with cabinet officials. If the administration of justice in this country is to be carried out in a nonpartisan, nonpolitical fashion, then Carter probably had more meetings with Griffin Bell in the first year of his presidency than was appropriate.

President Jimmy Carter's definition of politics is *not* "the authoritative allocation of values for a society," or "who gets what, when, and how." The president defined politics in Niebuhr's terms as *"the pursuit of justice in a sinful world."* Justice has always been an important concept for Carter. In a Law Day speech in Georgia before Carter kicked off his two-year presidential campaign, he spoke with some eloquence on the unequal justice that the criminal justice system has for the poor and for black citizens. On the campaign trail Carter promised a Justice Department that would not be "political" and he promised to put an end to executive lawlessness. Moreover, indicating some political naïveté, Carter promised to "never tell a lie" to the American people.

The performance of the Carter administration was somewhat uneven in the area of criminal justice. For example, the Justice Department indicted some of the FBI officials who had been responsible for the massive illegal domestic surveillance and harassment of antiwar groups in New York City during the late 1960s and early 1970s, yet in another action, the department also indicted Frank Snepp, the former CIA employee who broke his agreement of silence and wrote a book about the CIA performance in the withdrawal from Saigon during the fall of South Vietnam.

During the first two years of the Carter administration, the president appointed an old political friend, Griffin Bell, as attorney general. The Justice Department appeared to be relatively lax in the Bert Lance affair insofar as investigating potential illegalities, and the Justice Department carried out the successful plea bargain with former CIA Director Richard Helms on perjury charges. The charges grew out of Helms' testimony in regard to CIA involvement in the programs to destabilize the Allende regime in Chile.

Although the Carter administration restored at least a modicum of trust between citizens and the president in terms of executive lawlessness with his rhetoric about respect for the "rule of law," it is not clear whether Carter succeeded in depoliticizing the Department of Justice. Perhaps no president can truly accomplish this goal. Yet Carter's interaction activity with his later Attorney General Ben Civiletti more closely reflects the kind of nonmeeting activity that probably best serves the impartial administration of justice.

Although energy and education were important code words in the Carter domestic program, Carter did not meet very much with representatives from either department once these cabinet-level positions were formed. Table 2.4 also indicates very few meetings for health, education and welfare (later health and human services), and housing and urban development secretaries. Likewise, the secretaries of interior, transportation, commerce, labor, and agriculture did not rate very much interaction activity with President Carter.

Tables 2.5 and 2.6 show the rankings of advisors in terms of the numbers of meetings (interactions) with President Carter. Table 2.5 provides the top five advisors for each of the eight time periods to demonstrate how some advisors gain favor with the president during certain times and how other advisors drop out of presidential sight. No matter how one measures it, Brzezinski dominates the rankings of advisors during every time frame. He is never really challenged for access to the president. In the second half of 1977 Rosalynn Carter became a top-five advisor to the president as Bert Lance drops out of the government. By the end of the first half of 1978, Frank Moore, the congressional liaison for the Carter administration, emerges as an important advisor to the president.

In Table 2.6 one can see the overall rankings for the four-year period of 1977-81, and Brzezinski leads all advisors with 1,061 meetings with the president. Mondale just barely beat out Frank Moore for second place. Surprisingly, Rosalynn Carter finished in the top ten with one hundred official meetings with President Carter during the four years.

Tables 2.7 and 2.8 provide the pattern of activity from selected policy areas from 1977 to 1981 in the Carter administration. Table 2.7 shows the percentage of interactions with the president for five different policy areas during the eight different time frames. National security considerations were represented in 44 percent of the interactions at the beginning of the Carter administration and national security represented 46.4 percent of the interactions by the end of the Carter administration. Foreign policy never made up more than 10 percent of the interactions with a high point of 8.7 percent in the second half of 1978. Table 2.8 shows the overall

Table 2.5
Rankings of Advisors on Most Meetings with the President, 1977–81

1977	(1st half)	1977	(2nd half)
Name	Meetings	Name	Meetings
Brzezinski	157	Brzezinski	161
Mondale	60	Mondale	95
Lance	37	Vance	30
Turner	30	Schultze	30
Schultze	26	R. Carter	27

1978	(1st half)	1978	(2nd half)
Name	Meetings	Name	Meetings
Brzezinski	128	Brzezinski	123
Moore	66	Mondale	53
Mondale	46	Moore	42
Jordan	31	Jordan	37
Vance	23	Vance	36

1979	(1st half)	1979	(2nd half)
Name	Meetings	Name	Meetings
Brzezinski	126	Brzezinski	116
Moore	79	Moore	75
Mondale	64	Mondale	44
Jordan	35	McIntyre	29
McIntyre	30	Donovan	20

1980	(1st half)	1980-81	(2nd half)
Name	Meetings	Name	Meetings
Brzezinski	140	Brzezinski	110
Moore	88	Moore	57
Mondale	41	Brown	20
Donovan	29	Mondale	19
Jordan	26	Muskie	19
Brown	26		

Table 2.6
Overall Rankings of Advisors on Most Meetings with the President, 1977–81

Name	Total Meetings	Role
Brzezinski	1,061	National Security
Mondale	422	Vice-president
Moore	418	Congress Liaison
Brown	161	Department of Defense
Vance	155	State
Schultze	149	Economic Advisor
Jordan	148	Staff
McIntyre	139	OMB
Turner	131	CIA
R. Carter	100	Spouse

Table 2.7
Percent of Meetings with Advisors from Selected Policy Areas, 1977–81

Policy Area	Percent of Meetings(per year, first half and second half, rounded to nearest percent)							
	1977		1978		1979		1980-81	
	(1st)	(2nd)	(1st)	(2nd)	(1st)	(2nd)	(1st)	(2nd)
National Security	44	39	34	41	33	32	35	46
Foreign Policy	4	5	5	9	4	4	5	6
Staff Advice	26	30	39	36	42	42	44	39
Economic Advice	18	16	11	11	18	14	11	7
Domestic/ Cabinet	8	10	7	3	3	8	5	2

Table 2.8
Overall Rankings by Policy Areas, 1977–81

Policy Area	Meetings	Percentage of Total N equals 3,816
National Security Advice	1,455	38.0
Foreign Policy Advice	200	5.2
Staff Advice	1,412	37.0
Economic Advice	521	13.6
Domestic/Cabinet Advice	228	5.9

rankings for each policy area in terms of the number and percentage of interactions from 1977 to 1981 in official meetings with the president. National security advice finished first with 38 percent of the interactions and, surprisingly, foreign policy finished last with

5.2 percent of the interactions, as represented by meetings with the secretary of state and the ambassador to the United Nations.

Conclusions

President Carter, as is the case for American presidents since World War II, spent entirely too much time receiving and talking about national security matters in my opinion. National security should be one value among many that compete for valuable presidential time; it should not dominate presidential interactions in the advisory system. Moreover, Carter's national security advice was dominated by one person, Zbigniew Brzezinski, who probably was the most active national security advisor since Nixon's national security advisor, Dr. Henry Kissinger.

Table 2.9 shows the breakdown of presidential activity in formal meetings as measured by interactions with advisors from selected policy arenas.[14] While national security advisors made up 29.7 percent of all the interactions with the president, the U.N. ambassador made up .2 percent of the interactions. Most of this can be explained logistically. Brzezinski had an office in the White House and the ambassador to the United Nations was stationed in New York City. However, it would also seem that the president preferred to meet with close personal advisors like Brzezinski. The problem with such a preference revolves around the fact that presidents are only as good as their advisors. If most of the advice that the president hears centers around national security matters, then other equally important policy areas will suffer. Since it is difficult to believe that all things were running efficiently, without any problems, on the domestic level during the Carter administration, one has to question the systematic lack of advisory activity from domestic/cabinet level advisors and from economic advisors.

Over half of all interactions in the advisor system were between Carter and three people: Brzezinski, Mondale, and Moore. All other advisors had difficulty breaking into the interactions with the president. Only 1 percent of all the advisory interactions concerned the inflation fighters and only 1 percent of all the advisory interactions concerned the secretary of energy. If inflation and energy were key problems in the Carter administration, and most accounts maintain that this was the case, advisory interactions in these

Table 2.9
Presidential Activity in Selected Policy Areas, 1977–81

Rankings of Policy Area Advice	Percentage of Total Meetings, n = 3,816
1. National Security Advisors	29.7
2. Vice-president	11.0
3. Congressional Liaison	10.9
4. OMB Director	4.9
5. Secretary of State	4.9
6. Secretary of Defense	4.2
7. Council of Economic Advisors	3.9
8. White House Chief of Staff	3.8
9. Special Advisors to the President	3.6
10. CIA Director	3.4
11. Staff, Cabinet Meetings	3.0
12. Rosalynn Carter, Spouse	2.6
13. Secretary of Treasury	2.5
14. Domestic Policy, S. Eizenstat	1.8
15. Secretary of Energy	1.0
16. Inflation Fighters (Kahn, Bosworth)	1.0
17. Secretary of Labor	.9
18. Secretary of HEW/later HHS	.9
19. Secretary of Transportation	.8
20. NSC and Joint Chiefs	.7
21. Justice, Attorney General and FBI	.6
22. Secretary of Commerce	.5
23. Secretary of Agriculture	.5
24. Chair, Federal Reserve Board	.4
25. Secretary of Interior	.4
26. Secretary of HUD	.4
27. U.N. Ambassador	.3
28. Secretary of Education	.2
29. Office of Science and Technology	.1

areas were woefully inadequate. The situation was even worse in the areas of labor, health and human services, transportation, justice, commerce, agriculture, housing and urban development, interior, and education. Each of these areas made up less than 1 percent of advisory interactions.

NOTES

1. Graham Allison and Morton Halperin, "Bureaucratic Politics: A Paradigm and Some Policy Implications," *World Politics*, Spring 1972, p. 49.

2. Ibid.

3. Josiah Royce, in Paul Kurtz, ed., *American Thought before 1900* (New York: Macmillan, 1968), pp. 340-75, and see Herbert W. Schneider, *A History of American Philosophy* (New York: Columbia University Press, 1963), pp. 415-24, for discussions of Royce's loyalty-to-loyalty philosophy.

4. During the period from 1947 to 1953 Truman's loyalty progam investigated 4.75 million employees, of which 26,000 were cleared; 7,000 withdrew or resigned while under investigation. Only 560 people were removed or denied employment on loyalty charges. See Alfred Kelly and Winfred Harbison, *The American Constitution: Its Origins and Development* (New York: Norton, 1970), pp. 894-95.

5. Presumably this could be viewed as an early forerunner to Richard Nixon's "enemies list." In *Joint Anti-Fascist Committee v. McGrath* (1951) the Court allowed the group to remove their name from the attorney general's list since Truman's loyalty program had not authorized any subversive lists. Justices Black, Douglas, Frankfurter, and Jackson all attacked the constitutionality of such lists.

6. Truman Executive Order 10241, April 1951.

7. Eisenhower Executive Order 10450, April 1953; see Kelly and Harbison, *The American Constitution*, p. 895.

8. Irving Janis, *Victims of Groupthink* (Boston: Houghton Mifflin, 1972), pp. 197-98.

9. Hearings and Final Reports of the Select Committee to Study Government Operations with Respect to Intelligence Activities, U.S. Senate, 94th Congress, Vol. 1-7, and Final Report Books 1-5 (Church Committee).

10. Ibid.

11. See Jeb Magruder, *An American Life* (New York: Atheneum, 1974), and John Dean, *Blind Ambition* (New York: Simon & Schuster, 1976).

12. See Cyrus Vance, *Hard Choices* (New York: Simon & Schuster, 1983). For other perspectives on Carter foreign policy see Kenneth Oye et al., eds., *Eagle Entangled* (New York: Longman, 1979); Jimmy Carter, *Keeping Faith* (New York: Bantam Books, 1982); Hamilton Jordan, *Crisis* (New York: G. P. Putnam's Sons, 1982); Zbigniew Brzezinski, *Power and Principle* (New York: Farrar, Straus & Giroux, 1983); Charles Kegley and Eugene Wittkopf, eds., *Perspectives in American Foreign Policy* (New York: St. Martin's Press, 1983); Cecil Crabb and Pat Holt, *Invitation to Struggle* (Washington, D.C.: Congressional Quarterly Press, 1980); Gordon Hoxie, *Command Decision and the Presidency* (New York: Reader's Digest Press, 1977).

13. Rosalynn Carter, *First Lady of Plains* (Boston: Houghton Mifflin, 1984).

14. For sources relating to the domestic presidency and the Carter ad-

ministration see the following: Steve Wayne, *The Legislative Presidency* (New York: Harper & Row, 1978); Laurence Lynn and David Whitman, *The President as Policymaker* (Philadelphia: Temple Univeristy Press, 1981); David Davis, *Energy Politics* (New York: St. Martin's Press, 1982); Steven Shull and Lance LeLoup, eds., *The Presidency: Studies in Policy Making* (Brunswick, Ohio: King's Court Publishers, 1979); Paul Light, *President's Agenda: Domestic Policy Choice from Kennedy to Carter* (Baltimore: Johns Hopkins University Press, 1982); Steven Shull, *Domestic Policy Formation* (Westport, Conn.: Greenwood Press, 1983); Steven Shull, *Presidential Policy Making: An Analysis* (Brunswick, Ohio: King's Court Publishers, 1979); Ben Heineman and Curtis Hessler, *Memorandum to the President* (New York: Random House, 1981); Stuart Eizenstat, "A Democrat Looks at the Presidency," paper presented to the Annual Meeting of the American Political Science Association, New York, N.Y., September 5, 1981; and see Jeff Fishel, "Agenda Building in Presidential Campaigns: The Case of Jimmy Carter," paper presented to the Annual Meeting of the American Political Science Association, Washington, D.C., September 1-4, 1977.

3 | The Reagan Administration's Advisory Activity

The Reagan administration differed from the Carter administration in that more emphasis was put on staff advice, cabinet meetings, and national security council meetings in the Reagan administration. Moreover, Ronald Reagan's first year of his presidency was not dominated by any strong national security advisor to the degree that Brzezinski had dominated the Carter presidency.

Table 3.1 provides the raw data for numbers of interactions with the president. Reagan's foreign policy and national security advice interactions shows Reagan did not meet with advisors from these policy arenas as much as Carter did. Carter relied on meetings with CIA director Stansfield Turner much more than Reagan used William Casey. Carter met with Turner fifty three times during the first year whereas Reagan met with Casey only three times in 1981. Likewise, Carter met with his secretary of defense (Harold Brown) thirty seven times in his first year while Reagan officially interacted with Caspar Weinberger for only thirteen meetings.

The table also reveals that Reagan used staff advice, particularly advice and interactions from Jim Baker, Michael Deaver, and Edwin Meese much more than Carter relied on his staff in official meetings. Yet the Carter administration held thirty nine cabinet meetings in the first year while the Reagan administration held only twenty nine meetings. Reagan, however, was given media credit for reviving the use of the cabinet.

Even though the Reagan administration continued to maintain

Table 3.1
Reagan Advisory Patterns, 1981

Name	Meetings, 1981 1st half	2nd half	Total
NSC	16	17	33
R. Allen	101	17	118
A. Haig	18	18	36
C. Weinberger	6	7	13
J. Kirkpatrick	0	2	2
W. Casey	1	2	3
Generals, JCS	3	2	5
Staff	101	100	201
J. Baker	9	10	19
M. Deaver	4	9	13
E. Meese	11	9	20
Cabinet	17	12	29
G. Bush	52	13	65
E. Dole	2	0	2
M. Friedersdorf	1	0	1
Environment Group	0	3	3
K. Khachigian	4	0	4
Economic Group	7	4	11
M. Baldridge	6	2	8
P. volcker	2	2	4
M. Weidenbaum	12	7	19
D. Regan	17	13	30
D. Stockman	19	10	29
R. Schweiker	2	0	2
S. Pierce	1	0	1
T. Bell	1	0	1
D. Lewis	3	4	7
R. Donovan	4	1	5
J. Watt	1	1	2
J. Edwards	2	0	2
J. Block	5	0	5
A. Gorsuch	1	0	1
W. Webster	2	0	2
W. Smith	3	1	4
Totals	434	266	700

that Vice-President Bush had a stronger relationship with President Reagan than even Walter Mondale had with Carter, the number of meetings between Bush and Reagan does not indicate that Bush had a stronger, more active relationship. Mondale met with Carter 155 times in the first year while Bush officially interacted with Reagan for only 65 meetings.

Table 3.1 also shows that Reagan did not have as many interactions with economic advisors as Carter did in his first year as president (see Table 2.3). Carter had 180 economic interactions with advisors while Reagan only had 101 interactions. Carter also relied on domestic/cabinet level advice and interaction much more than Reagan. Carter had 94 interactions in this area (see Table 2.4) as compared to Reagan's 32 interactions in this area.

Table 3.2 provides a breakdown of meetings/interactions with the president by ranking advisors who had the most access to the president during the first half of the year and the second half of the year. Clearly, staff meetings dominated the Reagan presidency, while meetings with the national security advisor dominated the Carter presidency.

Table 3.3 indicates the breakdown of the interactions with the president with respect to various policy areas and it shows that the Reagan administration in its first year did not have as many meetings with advisors as the Carter administration. Carter had 1,055 meetings with advisors in his first year and Reagan met with advisors 708 times.

By looking at Table 2.8 and comparing Carter's overall breakdowns by policy areas to Reagan's first-year breakdowns, one can see that about 38 percent of all of Carter's interactions came from national security advisors while Reagan had 24.3 percent of his interactions in that area. The number of interactions with foreign policy advisors was remarkably similar for both presidents with Reagan having 5.4 percent of his interactions in this area compared to Carter's 5.2 percent. Likewise, the reliance on economic advice and domestic cabinet-level advice took up about the same percentages of interactions in both presidencies. However, the administrations differed significantly in reliance upon staff advice, with Reagan's staff advice taking up 51.5 percent of his interactions in the first year and Carter's taking up 37 percent.

IS REAGAN AN ACTIVE OR PASSIVE PRESIDENT?

There seems to be disagreement in the scholarly literature as to whether Ronald Reagan is an active or passive president. James Barber, in his classic work *The Presidential Character*, said presidents could be placed on a continuum of activity-passivity by ask-

Table 3.2
Rankings of Advisors on Most Meetings with President Reagan, 1981

Name	1st-half meetings	Name	2nd-half meetings
1. R. Allen	101	1. Staff	100
2. Staff	101	2. A. Haig	18
3. G. Bush	52	3. NSC	17
4. D. Stockman	19	4. R. Allen	17
5. A. Haig	18	5. G. bush	13
6. Cabinet	17	6. D. Regan	13
7. D. Regan	17	7. Cabinet	12
8. NSC	16	8. J. Baker	10
9. M. Weidenbaum	12	9. D. Stockman	10
10. E. Meese	11	10. E. Meese	9
		11. M. Deaver	9

Table 3.3
Percent of Meetings with Advisors from Selected Policy Areas, 1981

Policy Area	1st half n	1st half percentage	2nd half n	2nd half percentage	Total n	Total percentage
National Security	127	29.1	45	16.6	172	24.3
Foreign Policy	18	4.1	20	7.3	38	5.4
Staff Advice	204	46.6	161	59.4	365	51.5
Economic Advice	63	14.4	38	14.0	101	14.3
Domestic/ Cabinet	25	5.7	7	2.6	32	4.5
Totals	437		271		708	

ing, "How much energy does the man invest in his presidency?"[1]
In the *New York Times*, in September 1980, Barber labeled Reagan as a "passive-positive" character type, which indicated that Barber had placed Reagan on the passive side of the activity-passivity baseline.[2] Richard Watson and Norman Thomas observed

Reagan's behavior and concluded, "In his first year in office he was an activist president, successfully courting the Congress and American people on behalf of his ambitious new program of budget and tax cuts."[3]

One problem in the discussion is how one measures the energy invested by a president in his presidency. Barber did not provide empirical measures to help scholars place presidents on the activity-passivity baseline in his book, as James Qualls has observed in a controversial article.[4] Theodore Macaluso, in his empirical test of presidential character and presidential action, looked at vetoes, proposed governmental reorganization plans, and nominations sent to the Senate as evidence of presidential activity.[5] Yet it was William Lammers who showed students of the American presidency an empirical and comparative way to look at presidential activity. Lammers used the *Public Papers of the Presidents* from Hoover to Carter to examine attention-focusing activities of presidents.[6] Lammers looked at public addresses, Washington-area appearances, White House public activities, and political travel as indicators of presidential activity.

This chapter will compare the presidential activity of Ronald Reagan with Jimmy Carter, a president that most scholars clearly consider to have been active, across a broad range of activity as revealed in the *Public Papers of the Presidents*. Whether the Carter administration provided an "open presidency" after the Watergate years is still a debatable proposition. However, one fact is not in doubt. The records of the Carter administration as provided in his public papers show for the first time a detailed account of the scheduled meetings that Carter had each day. The Reagan administration continued this practice of publishing the president's meeting schedule thus allowing for some interesting comparisons.

Methods

To measure presidential activity within the Reagan and Carter administrations, the same process used in chapter 2 of counting interactions was used.

Meetings and interactions between the president and principal policy advisors were recorded from the national security area, the foreign policy area, staff, domestic policy, and the economic advice area. Interactions with advisors were recorded in five different time frames from each presidency. These time frames correspond to the publication volumes of the *Public Papers of the President*. Carter's interactions were recorded from January through June 1977, July through December 1977, January through June 1978, July through December 1978, and January through June 1979. Reagan's five time frames were January through June, 1981, July through December, 1981, January through June 1982, July through December 1982, and January through June 1983.

Yet the president does more than just hold meetings with advisors and members of his administration. This research also looks at the various forms of presidential activity that require an investment of the president's energy into his presidency. The president signs bills and makes bill-signing remarks. He gives executive orders and makes proclamations and official statements. He sends memoranda to federal agencies and makes appointments and nominations. The president engages in political communications by making addresses, remarks, and messages. Moreover, he gives addresses to the nation and attends official party meetings and fundraising dinners. He gives news conferences and travels to domestic cities and foreign nations.

The president engages in communications with Congress by sending letters and messages. He communicates decisions like budget rescissions and deferrals, and he sends veto messages. The president also interacts with members of the House and the Senate when he invites congressional leaders to the White House for meetings.

The president must engage in symbolic activities to conduct the American presidency. He attends ceremonies and plays national host to some groups. He is also lobbied by minority groups and by special interest groups that have a certain policy approach. The president must see governors, state and local officials, mayors, and members of the judiciary. He receives national policy reports and sees party officials. The president may want to invite members of the media to a working lunch. Finally, the president visits heads of state and sees foreign dignitaries and U.S. as well as foreign ambassadors.

These are the kinds of tasks that make up the modern American presidency as revealed by the *Public Papers of the President*. Thus it is possible to compare quantitatively in how much of each activity Carter and Reagan invested their energies.

Problems

This method of measuring energy expended by Reagan and Carter has its problems. As seen in chapter 2, *Public Papers of the Presidents* does not reveal what was discussed at the meetings and they do not indicate how long each meeting lasted. There is also no way to tell whether the president was participating in the meeting. Perhaps the president was napping during the scheduled meeting.

Other presidential activities do not require much presidential energy. It is not too taxing to sign one's name to a bill or to forward a message to Congress which the staff has prepared. Yet for all these empirical problems, the fact that Reagan and Carter both published a schedule of their activities allows one to gauge the energy expended in their presidencies.

Participants in Reagan Administration Meetings, 1981

Allen, Richard, Assistant to the President for National Security Affairs.

Baker, James, Chief of Staff.

Baldridge, Malcolm, Secretary of Commerce.

Bell, Terrel, Secretary of Education.

Block, John, Secretary of Agriculture.

Bush, George, Vice President.

Casey, William, Director of the Central Intelligence Agency.

Deaver, Michael, Deputy Chief of Staff.

Dole, Elizabeth, Assistant to the President for Public Liaison.

Donovan, Raymond, Secretary of Labor.

Edwards, James, Secretary of Energy.

Friedersdorf, Max, Assistant to the President for Legislative Affairs.

Gorsuch, Ann, Administrator of Environmental Protection Agency.

Haig, Alexander, Secretary of State.

Khachigian, Ken, Speechwriter.

Kirkpatrick, Jeanne, Ambassador to the United Nations.

Lewis, Andrew, Secretary of Transportation.

Meese, Edwin, Counsellor to the President.

Pierce, Samuel, Secretary of Housing and Urban Development.

Regan, Donald, Secretary of Treasury.

Schweiker, Richard, Secretary of Health and Human Services.

Smith, William, Attorney General.

Stockman, David, Director of the Office of Management and Budget.

Volcker, Paul, Chairman of the Federal Reserve Board.

Watt, James, Secretary of Interior.

Weidenbaum, Murray, Chairman of the Council of Economic Advisors.

Weinberger, Caspar, Secretary of Defense.

Results

American presidents expend energy in their presidencies by attending scheduled meetings with various advisors from their administration. Table 3.4 indicates that Jimmy Carter was clearly more active than Ronald Reagan in this respect. Carter had meetings and interactions 2,498 times compared to Reagan's 1,345. Most of this difference can be explained by Carter's practice of meeting almost every day with national security advisor Zbigniew Brzezinski. Reagan continued this practice in his first six months of his presidency by meeting almost daily with Richard Allen, his national security advisor. Later Reagan dropped this practice and relied on a one-page memo from his national security advisor William Clark. Carter as seen in Table 3.4 was more active in national security, foreign policy, staff–vice-president–Cabinet, economic, and domestic policy meetings than Reagan.

Carter had seven people who tallied over one hundred interactions with him during the thirty-month period from January 1977 to July 1979. He met with Brzezinski 695 times; Vice-President Walter Mondale 318 times; Frank Moore, congressional liaison, 198 times; staff–Hamilton Jordan 124 times; Charles Schultze–Council of Economic Advisors 114 times; and CIA Director Stansfield Turner 111 times.[7]

Reagan had only six people score over fifty interactions with him from January 1981 through June 1983. He had 492 staff meetings;

national security advisor Richard Allen had 118 meetings; Vice-President George Bush had 96 meetings; the National Security Council scored 85 meetings; the secretary of state, first Alexander Haig and then George Shultz, tallied 68 meetings; and the cabinet met 66 times.

With respect to policy breakdowns, Carter tallied 38.8 percent of his meetings in the national security arena, 5.4 percent in foreign policy, 34.4 percent with staff, 15.0 percent with economic advisors, and 6.3 percent on domestic policy. Reagan, on the other hand, spent 20.1 percent of his interactions in national security, 6.5 percent in foreign policy, 56.8 percent with staff, 11.4 percent in the economic arena, and 5.1 percent on domestic policy.

Thus, Carter clearly conducted more substantive meetings during the thirty-month period than did Reagan. Reagan was not as active in policy meetings as Carter was.

Table 3.5 indicates the amount of activity in official presidential communications. This measure is not a true measure of presidential energy expended; rather it shows how much energy is expended by the Carter administration and the Reagan administration. It is assumed that the Carter staff and the Reagan staff processed these official presidential communications, so that a president would have only to sign his name. Yet even in this category of presidential activity, Carter tallied more official presidential communications than Reagan.

However, Reagan was not inactive in these areas. He scored more bill-signing remarks and communications to Congress than Carter did. He had more rescission, deferral, and veto messages combined than Carter did. He had more proclamations and official statements than Carter. Carter showed more activity than Reagan in executive orders, memos to federal agencies, appointments, and nominations. Thus, in this second aspect of the official presidential activity, Carter scored more communications than the "Great Communicator" Ronald Reagan.

Thus far, Carter appears to have been more active than Reagan. Yet Table 3.6 on political activities indicates that Reagan was more active than Carter by a score of 1,788 to 1,399. Reagan scored more addresses, remarks, and messages than Carter. He had more addresses on radio and television than Carter, and he had more fund-raisers. He even had more meetings with minorities during

Table 3.4
Carter, Reagan Administration Meetings

Area	President C=Carter R=Reagan	Meetings per Six-month Time Frames					Totals
		1st	2nd	3rd	4th	5th	
National	C	206	228	180	181	174	971
Security	R	127	45	32	38	28	270
Foreign	C	19	31	25	38	21	134
Policy	R	18	20	19	19	12	88
Staff, VP,	C	121	174	185	158	221	859
Cabinet	R	204	161	149	121	130	765
Economic	C	86	94	51	49	97	377
Advice	R	63	38	11	24	17	153
Domestic	C	37	57	33	12	18	157
Policy	R	25	7	13	5	19	69
Totals	C	471	584	474	438	531	2498
	R	437	271	224	207	206	1345

Table 3.5
Official Presidential Communications (Thirty-Month Period)

Type	Carter	Reagan
Bill-signing Remarks and Communications to Congress	577	803
Recisions, Deferrals and Veto Messages	35	44
Executive Orders	187	143
Proclamations	187	254
Statements	238	250
Memos to Federal Agencies	137	35
Appointments, Nominations	2,307	1,423
Totals	3,668	2,952

Table 3.6
Political Activities (Thirty-Month Period)

Type	Carter	Reagan
Addresses, Remarks, Messages	552	885
Addresses to Nation Television or Radio	7	71
Party Meetings	14	9
Fund-raisers	13	15
News Conferences	50	19
Domestic Travel, Cities	160	102
Foreign Travel, Nations	51	18
Minorities Meetings	46	54
Presidential Ceremonies	101	112
White House Host Events	54	94
Publishers' Meetings	37	6
U.S. Ambassadors' Meetings	42	81
Foreign Ambassadors' Meetings	55	88
Foreign Heads of State	66	50
Special Interest Groups	161	184
Totals	1,399	1,788

his first thirty months in office than Carter did. He took part in more presidential ceremonies, hosted more White House events, and met more U.S. and foreign ambassadors than Carter did. He was even lobbied more by special interest groups than Carter was.

Carter scored more party meetings in his political activities than Reagan and he had more news conferences than Reagan. Carter scored more domestic and foreign travel than Reagan. Moreover,

Carter scored more meetings with publishers and more meetings with foreign heads of state than Reagan.

This surprising Table 3.6 indicates that in political activities Reagan is not a passive president. With respect to intergovernmental and party interaction in the White House, President Reagan was active in trying to turn on his charm. Table 3.7 indicates that Reagan met more with members of the House and Senate than Carter did. Moreover, Reagan scored more meetings with governors, mayors, and local and state officials than Carter. Carter met more with judicial and party officials and took more national policy reports than Reagan. Reagan clearly was more active than Carter in this important area of political meetings.

Conclusions

By looking at the four categories of presidential meetings and interactions in the four tables, Carter is more active overall than Reagan. Carter scored 8,261 interactions while Reagan scored 7,041

Table 3.7
Intergovernmental/Party Interactions in White House Meetings
(Thirty-Month Period)

Type	Carter	Reagan
Congressional Meetings	565	720
Governors' Meetings	46	100
Mayors/Local Officials	24	58
State Officials	9	56
Judicial Officials	9	3
National Policy Reports	10	3
Party Officials	33	16
Totals	696	956

interactions. Thus Barber would be correct in categorizing Carter as more active than Reagan. Reagan is 85.2 percent as active as Carter in terms of presidential interactions.

If one looks at combined results in Tables 3.4 and 3.5, which look at official presidential interactions, Carter scored 6,166 interactions to Reagan's 4,298 interactions. Here, Reagan is only 69.7 percent as active as Carter and he could be labeled as a passive *official* president.

However, if one looks at the political presidency as seen in Tables 3.6 and 3.7, Reagan emerges as the more active president. Carter scored 2,095 interactions and Reagan 2,744. Thus, Carter was only 76.3 percent as active as Ronald Reagan in the political presidency.

This new empirical evidence provides ammunition for both sides of the argument regarding whether Reagan is an active or passive president. Reagan can probably best be labeled as a politically active president who is much less active in the official presidency. Carter, on the other hand, was an active president in the official presidency and less active in the political presidency.

THE PRESIDENT AND INTEREST GROUP ACCESS

As American political life has become more complex over the years and as interest groups have become more organized, the White House has become a focal point for activities of interest groups. Interest group activity to lobby the president has become a "virtually permanent feature" of the modern presidency since Franklin Roosevelt, according to Joseph Pika.[8] Since the American president has come to play an increasingly important role in the public policy process, interest groups and their lobbyists now descend on the presidency with the same vigor as they descend on Congress. In terms of representation, this puts the American president in a contradictory position. He must represent all of the American people at the same time he is asked to represent the interests of certain groups in American political life.

The most important resource that an interest group can have in dealing with the American president is *access*. One kind of access has become institutionalized in the form of the Office of Public Liaison.[9] This allows various interest groups to have access to White

House staff members who are assigned the responsibility of handling a specific group's exchanges. The number of group liaison assignments on the White House staff and the number of mixed liaison portfolios has increased over the past fifty years.[10] The interest group then must hope that their particular staff liaison represents their concerns to the president. They must hope that their liaison is an experienced bureaucratic politics fighter and that he has much influence within the inner circles of the presidency. As John Kessel has noted, however, these staff liaison positions are of limited organizational importance within the executive branch of government.[11] The other kind of access to the American president is direct access in face-to-face meetings with the president. Here groups can be sure that the president is hearing their exchange. Since presidential time is so valuable, it becomes important for interest groups to develop the ability to gain direct access to the president.

Methods

In 1977 the Carter administration began publishing the daily meetings of the president and the Reagan administration has continued this practice. Thus it is possible to compare administrations in terms of interest group access. This research looks at meetings held by President Jimmy Carter during the first half of 1977 until June 30, 1979, and the meetings held by President Ronald Reagan during the first half of 1981 until June 30, 1983. The frequencies of interaction just measures access. It cannot measure interest group success in achieving its objectives since no record of the meeting is available at this time. A measure of access is important because it reveals that some groups are more equal than others.

Results

As Table 3.8 indicates, the Carter administration had a disproportionate amount of meetings with black interest groups. Carter met with black groups thirty times over a two-and-one-half-year period, making blacks the minority group with the most access to the Carter administration. Next came Jews and feminists with four meetings each followed by Hispanics with three meetings and na-

Table 3.8
Carter Interaction with Minorities, 1977–79

Group	Meetings per Year (first half and second half)					Totals
	1977 (1st)	(2nd)	1978 (1st)	(2nd)	1979 (1st)	
Blacks	4	8	4	10	4	30
Hispanics	3	0	0	0	0	3
Jews	1	1	1	0	1	4
Arabs	0	1	0	0	0	1
Indians/ Native Americans	0	0	1	1	0	2
Greeks	0	0	1	0	0	1
Elderly	0	1	0	0	0	1
Women/ Feminists	1	1	0	1	1	4
Totals	9	12	7	12	6	46

tive American Indians with two meetings. Arab groups, Greeks, and the elderly had only one meeting each. The black community had been an important electoral group in Carter's winning 1976 coalition and the Carter administration tried to continue to see black interest group support during the Carter presidency. However, this goal seems to have been pursued at the exclusion of most other minority groups in American political society as seen in Table 3.8.

The Reagan administration on the other hand did not allow the black community as much access to President Reagan as was the case in the Carter administration. Table 3.9 shows that Reagan met with black groups at the early stages of his administration to try to establish a dialogue. However, by July 1, 1982, the access was closed entirely. The leading minority in the Reagan coalition was

Table 3.9
Reagan Interaction with Minorities, 1981–83

Group	Meetings (per year, first half and second half)					
	1981 (1st)	(2nd)	1982 (1st)	(2nd)	1983 (1st)	Totals
Blacks	9	4	6	0	0	19
Hispanics	21	0	1	0	1	23
Jews	2	1	1	0	0	4
Poles	0	3	1	1	0	5
Italians	0	1	0	0	0	1
Ethnics Unspecified	1	1	0	0	0	2
Elderly	0	1	0	0	0	1
Totals	33	11	9	1	1	55

the Hispanic community. Reagan met with Hispanic/Latino interest groups more than any other group. Most of these meetings were in the first six months of his administration as Reagan tried to thank as many Hispanic groups as possible for their valuable electoral support in the 1980 presidential election.

After Hispanics, Reagan met most often with black groups, nineteen times. He met with Polish groups five times and with Jewish groups four times during this thirty-month period. At the bottom of the list, Reagan met with unspecified ethnics twice and once each with elderly and Italian groups. He did not meet with any Arab groups, Indians, Greeks, or feminists. After his first six months, Reagan drastically curtailed access to minorities as his decreasing level of activity indicates. From July 1, 1982, to June 30, 1983, he met with only two minority groups. After his initial thanks for electoral support, the Reagan administration became a place where minority groups could not lobby the president in person. This was in keeping with Reagan's rhetoric about being a president for all of the American people and not a president who was tied down to narrow minority group interests. For example, feminists who complained about the little access to the Carter White House soon found out that it was better than the access provided them by the Reagan administration. As Bruce Miroff has noted, "In its relationship with social movements the White House is concerned with appearances as well as actions. The White House naturally shies away from too close a symbolic link with a controversial social movement, lest it alienate other supporters."[12]

In theory, American presidents talk as if they are presidents of "all the people," but as Kathy B. Smith has observed, "The definition of the whole nation and all the people is, in the final analysis, a personal decision of each president within the socio-political context of his time."[13]

With respect to public policy, this personal political decision can be seen in the types of groups given access by Carter and the types of groups given access by Reagan. Table 3.10 indicates that Carter's direct interaction with interest groups was characterized by a high frequency of contact with labor unions. Carter met with unions thirty five times during this thirty-month period. Next in the Carter schema of access came military and veterans groups with twenty four meetings. Carter met twenty one times with elements from the liberal coalitions in the form of public interest groups, environmental groups, and consumer groups. Moreover, Carter as a born-again Christian also met with religious groups twenty one times. He met with corporate leaders sixteen times and he talked with educational interests twelve times. At the bottom of the list of Carter special interest meetings were national business groups with eight meetings, professional associations with eight meetings, farmers with six meetings, small business and arts/humanities groups with four each, and bankers with three meetings. In all, Carter met with twelve different types of interest groups for some 162 meetings. His activity showed an up-and-down trend, but by the second half of 1978, Carter's interest group meeting activity had significantly dropped off.

The Reagan administration emphasized different groups in deciding who would get to see the president. In his rhetoric, Reagan has criticized the government by interest groups, and as Mark Peterson and Jack Walker have maintained, "The [Reagan] administration believes that to permanently reduce the size of the federal

Table 3.10
Carter Interaction with Interest Groups, 1977–79

Group	Meetings (per year, first and second half)					
	1977 (1st)(2nd)		1978 (1st)(2nd)		1979 (1st)	Totals
Unions	12	6	13	2	2	35
Military/Vets	8	2	7	5	2	24
Humanities/ Arts	1	0	1	2	0	4
Farmers	1	1	2	2	0	6
Small Business	1	0	1	0	2	4
Bankers	2	0	1	0	0	3
Professional Associations	5	1	1	1	0	8
Education	3	2	4	0	3	12
Corporate Leaders	3	4	5	2	2	16
Business	1	1	5	0	1	8
Public Interest	6	5	6	0	4	21
Religious	8	4	1	5	3	21
Totals	51	26	47	19	19	162

establishment—the president's fundamental, overriding goal—the number of interest groups must be reduced."[14] Yet as Table 3.11 indicates, Ronald Reagan met with special interest groups even more than Jimmy Carter!

Reagan met with corporate leaders more than any other special interest group during the thirty-month period. His forty two meetings with these corporate leaders showed that Reagan restructured interest group access rather than abolishing it. The next group to

Table 3.11
Reagan Interaction with Interest Groups, 1981–83

Group	Meetings(per year, first and second half)					
	1981 (1st)(2nd)		1982 (1st)(2nd)		1983 (1st)	Totals
Unions	10	3	2	0	3	18
Military/ Vets	2	1	8	0	3	14
Humanities/ Arts	1	0	0	1	0	2
Farmers	15	1	1	0	0	17
Small Business	0	1	3	1	1	6
Professional Associations	1	2	1	0	2	6
Education	1	3	3	3	7	17
Corporate Leaders	1	10	11	12	8	42
Business	5	2	1	1	1	10
Public Interest	0	0	0	0	0	0
Religious	2	9	1	4	5	21
Conservative, Right-Wing	22	1	3	0	4	30
Totals	60	33	34	22	34	183

have access to the president was the conservative, right-wing category. Reagan met with these groups thirty times, compared to no meetings with these groups for Carter. To continue this restructuring of interests in terms of presidential access, Reagan did not meet with any public interest, consumer, or environmental groups during this thirty-month period. Reagan's third favorite group to see were religious groups with twenty one meetings. Next came unions with eighteen meetings and farmers and educational groups with seventeen meetings each. In all, Reagan met with twelve different categories of groups for some 183 meetings.

Conclusions

This research has indicated that the interest group system is alive and well at the White House. It has not been terminated in the Reagan administration, it has just been restructured. Corporate leaders, conservative, right-wing groups, and religious groups dominate the access channels to President Ronald Reagan whereas unions, military and veterans groups, public interest–consumer–environmental groups, and religious groups dominated the access channels of the Carter administration. While black groups were the dominant minority interest group with access to Jimmy Carter, they have been replaced by Hispanics/Latinos as the dominant minority group with access to Ronald Reagan. Given the complexities of modern American politics, presidents must continue to allow their doors to be open to interest groups. Yet is is a personal political decision that each president makes when he decides who will have access and how much access any group may have. Finally, the president may even decide to close the door to certain groups in the name of wanting to serve all of the people at the same time he is allowing other groups the benefit of a direct meeting with him.

NOTES

1. James Barber, *The Presidential Character*, 3d ed. (Englewood Cliffs N.J.: Prentice Hall, 1985), p. 8.
2. Ibid. pp. 464-467.
3. Richard Watson and Norman Thomas, *The Politics of the Presidency* (New York: Wiley, 1983), p. 406.
4. James Qualls, "Barber's Typological Analysis of Political Leaders," *American Political Science Review*, vol. 71 (March 1977).
5. Theodore Macaluso, "The Presidential Character and Presidential Action in Conflict Situations: An Event Series Analysis," paper given at Annual Meeting of the Southern Political Science Association, Atlanta, Georgia, November 4–6, 1976.
6. William Lammers, "Presidential Attention-Focusing Activities," in

Doris Graber, ed., *The President and the Public* (Philadelphia: Institute for Study of Human Issues, 1982), pp. 145-71.

7. See John Kessel, *Presidential Parties* (Homewood, Ill.: Dorsey Press, 1984). He draws the conclusion that William Clark was more influential in the Reagan White House than Zbigniew Brzezinski was in the Carter White House. This assertion is clearly wrong. Kessel's data were gathered from October 1980 to March 1981 for the Carter administration and during the summer of 1982 for the Reagan administration, as stated on page 590 of his book. This time frame is not sufficient to gather data on White House influence, especially since Carter was a lame duck president from November 1980 to January 1981.

8. Joseph Pika, "Interest Groups and the White House: Comparing Administrations," paper delivered at the Annual Meeting of the American Political Science Association, New Orleans, Louisiana, August 29 to September 1, 1985, p. 2.

9. Martha J. Kumar and Michael B. Grossman, "The Presidency and Interest Groups," in Michael Nelson, ed., *The Presidency and the Political System* (Washington, D.C.: Congressional Quarterly Press, 1984), p. 285.

10. Joseph Pika, "Interest Groups and the Executive," in A. Cigler and B. Loomis, eds., *Interest Group Politics* (Washington, D.C.: Congressional Quarterly Press, 1983), p. 317 and see pp. 30-31.

11. John Kessel, *Presidential Parties* (Homewood Ill.: Dorsey Press, 1984), p. 151.

12. Bruce Miroff, "Presidential Leverage over Social Movements," *Journal of Politics*, vol. 43 (1981), p. 14.

13. Kathy B. Smith, "The Representative Role of the President," *Presidential Studies Quarterly*, vol. 11, no. 2 (Spring 1981), p. 207.

14. Mark Peterson and Jack Walker, "The Impact of the First Reagan Administration upon the National Interest Group System," paper delivered at the Annual Meeting of the American Political Science Association, New Orleans, Louisiana, August 31, 1985, p. 1.

4 | Evaluating Macho Presidents and Presidential Greatness

American presidential politics allows grown men to play numerous games to show off their manhood. The election of the American president provides for a competition that is like the "Superbowl" of politics. Candidates engage in sporting behavior to establish winners and losers. The media adds to the excitement by covering American presidential politics like a sports event. The media report who is ahead, who is behind, who looks strong, who looks weak, and how it will probably end up. In American presidential politics, winning is the only thing. Americans build superheroes out of ordinary individuals who happen to win a presidential election and they castigate the people who lose elections.

The macho presidential style places the ability to portray strength, aggressiveness, and power at the top of its demands. The great president is usually the president who tries to expand his powers or acts as an activist. The presidents who engage in successful wars are remembered highly and the president who tries to become a strong leader is valued.

As Clinton Rossiter has noted, "ranking the presidents" has always been a favorite indoor sport of history-minded Americans.[1] The game can be played with Reagan, Carter, and Ford as well as with the Roosevelts, Truman, and Eisenhower. Under some circumstances the game attempts to go behind pure subjectivity, but this state of events is too rare. Some scholars have tried to provide some criteria for presidential greatness academic games, and Rossiter's yardsticks are helpful. Rossiter believed that when judging presidential performance, one should look at the following yardsticks:

1. In what sort of times did the president live? A man cannot be judged a great president unless he lived in great times. For example, Washington lived at the start of the nation and Jackson lived during the upsurge of democracy. Lincoln served during the Civil War and Wilson and Franklin Roosevelt served during world wars.

2. If the times were great, how bravely and imaginatively did the president bear the burden of extraordinary responsibility? Was he a man of strength and independence or was he indifferent?

3. What was his philosophy of presidential power? To be a great president one must be an activist.

4. What sort of governmental technician was he?

5. How efficiently did he organize his energies, direct his lieutenants and thus exercise power?

6. On what kind of people did he call for help?

7. What manner of man was beneath the trappings of the office?

8. What was his influence on the presidency?

9. What was his influence on history? In particular, did he inspire or represent and find words to explain some earth-shaking readjustment in the pattern of American society?

Moreover, Rossiter reminds us of one important fact in rating presidents:

American history is written, if not always made, by men of moderate views, broad interests and merciful judgments. Time works for, rather than against most presidents. The men who write texts for our great-grandchildren, like the men who wrote them for us, will be concerned with broad accomplishments and failures, not with petty tales of corruption, ill temper and intrigue.[2]

In his particular rankings, Rossiter found that from Washington to Eisenhower only eight presidents performed *great* jobs: George Washington, Thomas Jefferson, Andrew Jackson, Abraham Lincoln, Theodore Roosevelt, Woodrow Wilson, Franklin Roosevelt, and Harry Truman. In the creditable category, Rossiter listed Grover

Cleveland, James Polk, Dwight Eisenhower, Rutherford B. Hayes, John Adams, and Andrew Johnson. Average performers, according to Rossiter, included John Quincy Adams, Martin Van Buren, John Tyler, Chester Arthur, William McKinley, William Taft, and Herbert Hoover. As for those who rated an "irresponsible sort of exercise" of job performance, he included James Madison, James Monroe, Millard Fillmore, Benjamin Harrison, and Calvin Coolidge. Under insufficient data for ranking, Rossiter named William Henry Harrison, Zachary Taylor, and James Garfield. Finally, in worst performance, he listed Franklin Pierce, James Buchanan, Ulysses S. Grant, and Warren Harding.

Rossiter's guidelines provide areas that presidential raters should be concerned about, but they do not specify what quality performance and competence in each area are. Robert DiClerico has been a student of presidential grading for some time and he has contributed his own list of qualities needed for effective presidential leadership. For DiClerico an effective president must have:

1. empathy with the public

2. an ability to communicate

3. credibility

4. a sense of timing

5. courage

6. decisiveness

7. vision

8. flexibility

9. a sense of power.[3]

Historian Thomas Bailey has also tried to contribute to understanding presidential greatness. He observes that some presidents have developed cults that attest to their greatness—for example, the Washington-Lincoln deification, the belated Jefferson canonization, the enshrinement of Wilson, the horseback heroes Jackson and Teddy Roosevelt, and the presidential martyr cults for Lincoln, Kennedy, and Franklin Roosevelt.[4]

Richard Neustadt made some inroads to a personality approach to rating presidents in his classic *Presidential Power* when he discussed the politics of leadership and the power to persuade.[5] Later, James Barber clearly outlined a theory from the personality aspects that influence presidential performance. Barber noted it would be possible to classify presidents according to the major dimensions of their presidential style. In Barber's attempt to classify leaders in pattern regularities he developed the theory of presidential style that claims "whatever works for the individual during the formative years after he has broken from his family will appear later to influence his presidential performance."[6] Barber evolved a labeling system that types each man according to his character (positive or negative) and his way of life (active or passive) to identify certain presidential types.[7] Dorothy Rudoni has developed an approach to presidential ranking that deals with "presidential perspective." Presidential perspective not only involves Barber's keen sense of personality involvement in the presidential assessment, but it involves the man's perception of the office and his responsibilities that guide his actual performance. Rudoni explained that "presidential perspective evolves with the thrust of political sensitivity and aspiration, and is directed by concept of office, use of institutional resources, and response to others."[8]

If an author were writing in the late 1950s and early 1960s, the student of the presidency more than likely would champion the strong liberal presidency. Candidate John Kennedy freely gave out this theoretical orientation toward presidential power on the campaign stump in 1960 when he said, "The president must place himself in the very thick of the fight. . . . He must be prepared to exercise the fullest powers of his office—*all that are specified and some that are not.*"[9] This view was supported by scholars like Richard Neustadt, Clinton Rossiter, and James M. Burns, among others. The notion that the president should be as strong as possible was a well-entrenched image in presidential scholarship.

If political scientists eulogized presidential power in the 1960s, the 1970s brought on a feeling of betrayal. As Erwin Hargrove noted:

The Bay of Pigs, the Vietnam War, and Watergate have taken the shine off of such an exercise (eulogizing presidential power). Our optimistic assumptions about the happy fusion of power and purpose have been exploded. It is not only that power has been abused but also that we trust too much in it.[10]

Strong presidents had been the hope of the future and in some circles they still are the hope of the future. In the 1960s presidents were believed, trusted, and worshipped. In the 1980s this description no longer fit.

If the 1960s and early 1970s saw presidential scholars engage in their favorite indoor sport of ranking presidents in terms of presidential greatness, then the 1980s have ushered in a new academic game that I call "presidential abominations." This new indoor game can be played with the same excitement that Thomas Bailey,[11] the Schlesinger polls,[12] and James Barber[13] had in playing presidential greatness games. In order to play one merely selects criteria and compares administrations for the quality and quantity of presidential wrongdoing. Playing a presidential ranking game that looks for manipulative executive behavior would have been unthinkable as late as the early 1960s when the office of the president was one of the most trusted and sacred American institutions. But the handling of the Indochina War, the Watergate experience, and the CIA-FBI revelations focused attention on manipulative behavior of presidents.

Nonetheless, during 1974 and 1975 a curious wave of Harry Truman nostalgia swept the country and the Truman revisionism still exists to some degree in the 1980s. In the first wave of Truman nostalgia, the rock group Chicago sang about Truman.[14] Merle Miller's oral biography of Harry Truman called *Plain Speaking*[15] made the best-seller lists during the Truman revival, and the actor James Whitmore toured the country doing a one-man play called "Give 'em Hell, Harry."[16] Songwriter Robert Lamm, when asked why he wrote about Truman, replied that after living through Nixon's presidency, he wanted to write a song about a president who told the truth. Senator Barry Goldwater in commenting on former President Gerald Ford's speech at Tulane University where Ford finally ended presidential commitments to South Vietnam said, "If we get a Harry Truman kind of leadership where the American people will rally around the president, then President Ford will be okay."[17]

The Truman nostalgia celebrated Truman because of his "honesty" and "openness." Many people in the 1970s perceived Truman to be one of the few American presidents to ever be truthful with the American people.[18] Whether Truman did or did not tell the American people the "truth" and about "what" is still an empirical question. Yet Senator Goldwater's notion that the American people rallied around Truman during his presidency to provide mass support does not stand up to close inspection. Goldwater's perception is not supported by public opinion and survey research data by any means.[19]

Students of the modern presidency were caught in an interesting analytical dilemma during the early post-Watergate revisionism in the mid-1970s over the concept "abuse of power." Richard Nixon's exercises of power as revealed through the Watergate investigations were labeled as "aberrations" by some observers, while other observers viewed the exercises of power as the culmination of a long train of presidential abuses of power. Where one stood with respect to these observations was often determined by:

1. one's definition of abuse of power
2. one's partisan political preferences
3. one's preference for a "strong" or "weak" president
4. one's view of what is ethically acceptable behavior
5. one's perceptions of what was understood to have happened in the Nixon administration
6. one's previous credentials in the art of Nixon-hating.

Efforts to resolve the dilemma were hindered by the fact that the intense Watergate investigations produced voluminous data on Nixon wrongdoing that blotted out perceptions of wrongdoing by previous administrations. But the CIA-FBI revelations of the mid-1970s gave presidential scholars more data to make comparisons between administrations.

A long list of formal and informal charges from the agenda of public controversy gathered against Nixon and they all related to abuse of power and presidential manipulation. Critics charged, with good evidence, that Nixon had used various governmental agencies for his own partisan political purposes and that he had engaged in illegal domestic activities like wiretapping and burglary. They argued that Nixon tried to muzzle dissent and that he used the CIA as a tool for his secret foreign policy. Moreover, Nixon and Henry Kissinger were accused of conducting the so-called secret bombing of Cambodia. Amid these charges, Nixon was asked to account for private wealth that he accumulated in office and to account for his fraudulent tax returns. Nixon was cited by some critics for manipulating political symbols when he had Kissinger announce one week before the 1972 election that "peace is at hand." Most important, the critics charged, Nixon had "covered up." The quintessential charge was that Nixon had lied to the American people. As Watergate evolved into its denouement, the validity of the charges against Nixon were beyond reproach.

Yet the dilemma of Nixon as "aberration" or Nixon as "culmination" is still unresolved. To resolve this question one would have to make judgments as to what extent other presidents engaged in (a) the use of bureaucracy for partisan political concerns, (b) the use of illegal domestic surveillance, (c) attempts to quiet dissent, (d) the use of CIA to meddle in the internal affairs of other nations, (e) the accumulation of personal wealth while in office, (f) symbolic manipulation, and (g) lying to the American people.

NEW CRITERIA FOR PRESIDENTIAL GREATNESS

As Richard Nixon's presidency continues to receive high marks during the historical revisionism of his presidency in the 1980s, it is important to evaluate the Nixon presidency during his "comeback." His book *The Real War* was published in 1980 and it read as a primer for the strong presidency. In an era when the United States was perceived by some as weak, as being kicked around abroad, as passive, and as uninterested in global responsibilities, Nixon wrote a book that championed a return to the strong presidency. According to Nixon presidents should:

1. Always be prepared to negotiate, but never negotiate without being prepared.

2. Never be belligerent, but always be firm.

3. Always remember that covenants should be openly agreed to but privately negotiated.

4. Never seek publicity that would destroy the ability to get results.

5. Never give up unilaterally what could be used as a bargaining chip. Make your adversaries give something for everything they get.

6. Never let your adversary underestimate what *you* would do in response to a challenge. Never tell him in advance what you would *not* do.

7. Always leave your adversary a face-saving line of retreat.

8. Always carefully distinguish between friends who provide some human rights and ememies who deny all human rights.

9. Always do at least as much for your friends as your adversaries do for your enemies.

10. Never lose faith. In a just cause faith can move mountains. Faith without strength is futile, but strength without faith is sterile.[20]

Nixon's advice on how presidents should behave was given some respectability by various presidential watchers. Most important, candidate Ronald Reagan adopted many of Nixon's principles for presidential behavior in his rhetoric on the campaign trail in 1980. Thus Nixon had made another incredible comeback from the role of disgraced, immoral imperial president of 1974 to the status of sage advisor to would-be presidents. By the 1980s much of Nixon's Watergate excesses had been forgotten and the idea of the strong presidency (as demonstrated by Nixon's leadership in foreign policy) was advocated by most serious presidential watchers.

Although Nixon is currently being reevaluated by some presidential raters to the category of "near great" or "great," it is difficult to believe that the raters have forgotten that this was the president who was responsible for widening the war in Indochina, overthrowing various governments, Watergate deception, and a clear disregard of U.S. constitutional processes. Perhaps the fact that a president like Nixon could emerge from the category of resigned president to near-great president testifies to the inadequate yardsticks that are currently used to measure presidential greatness. Alas, presidential greatness is in the eye of the beholder.

In order to evaluate presidential greatness and the strong presidency in terms other than characteristics from the macho presidential style, it is necessary to advance other guidelines that should be considered in evaluating presidential performance. Since criteria for presidential greatness is largely subjective, my criteria for great presidential performance fall along the following lines. A great president must have:

1. an adequate concept of justice—economic justice, political justice, and social justice.

2. a sincere commitment to the protection of U.S. civil liberties.

3. a commitment to the advancement of "human rights" and the promotion of better relations with underprivileged countries and their peoples.

4. a commitment to the promotion of U.S. civil rights for women, blacks, Indians, Chicanos, and others.

5. support for economic growth without support for the corporate domination of American society.

6. a concern for consumer protection and worker protection legislation in this country.

7. a commitment to clean up the environment and to promote environmental awareness.

8. a peace-loving nature and an antimilitaristic consciousness that promotes national security without promoting war.

9. nonpartisan leadership that does not give in to special interest in the economic realm.

10. an administration that has a minimal amount of political corruption and no self-aggrandizement.

Of course no American president has lived up to all of these guidelines and perhaps none could. Yet these are some of the concerns in American politics that can counter an oppresive macho presidential style or a runaway "strong president."

By using some of the guidelines advanced by Rossiter, Bailey, DiClerico, and others toward evaluating presidential greatness, and by using some of my guidelines, the following two chapters will attempt to evaluate the presidential performance of Jimmy Carter and Ronald Reagan's first term in office.

NOTES

1. Clinton Rossiter, *The American Presidency* (New York: Mentor Books, New American Library, 1962), pp. 138-39.

2. Ibid.

3. Robert DiClerico, *The American President*, 2d ed. (Englewood Cliffs, N.J.: Prentice-Hall, 1983), pp. 340-60.

4. Thomas Bailey, *Presidential Greatness* (New York: Appleton-Century-Crofts, 1966).

5. Richard E. Neustadt, *Presidential Power* (New York: John Wiley and Sons, 1960), p. 42.

6. James Barber, "The President's Analyst," *Time*, September 10, 1969, p. 58.

7. Ibid.

8. Dorothy Rudoni, "Presidential Perspective," mimeograph, Ball State University, 1972.

9. John Kennedy, speech to the National Press Club, January 14, 1960, in Elmer Cornwell, *The American Presidency: Vital Center* (Glenview, Illinois: Scott, Foresman, 1966), p. 19 (emphasis added).

10. Erwin Hargrove, "What Manner of Man? The Crisis of the Contemporary Presidency," in James Barber, ed., *Choosing the President* (Englewood Cliffs, N.J.: Prentice-Hall, 1974), p. 7.

11. Thomas Bailey, *Presidential Greatness* (New York: Appleton-Century-Crofts, 1966).

12. The Schlesinger Polls on Presidential Greatness, Arthur Schlesinger, Sr., "The U.S. Presidents," *Life* (November 1, 1948), p. 65 and Arthur Schlesinger, Sr. "Our Presidents: A Rating by 75 Historians," *New York Times Magazine*, July 29, 1962, pp. 12ff.

13. James Barber, *The Presidential Character* (Englewood Cliffs, N.J.: Prentice-Hall, 1972).

14. "Harry Truman," by Robert Lamm, from *Chicago VIII* album, Chicago Music, Inc. copyright Columbia Records 1975.

15. Merle Miller, *Plain Speaking: An Oral Biography of Harry Truman* (New York: Medallion, 1974).

16. In April 1975 President Gerald Ford attended Whitmore's opening show in Washington, D.C., and applauded the show. Of course Truman is one of Ford's presidential heroes.

17. Barry Goldwater interview, April 14, 1975, on ABC's "AM America," interviewed by Peter Jennings.

18. Paul Hagner finds this notion particularly disturbing. Hagner has a recording of Truman's announcement of the first atomic bombing of Hiroshima where Truman said to the American people, "Let the world note

today that the United States exploded the first atomic bomb on Hiroshima, *a military site."*

19. John Mueller, *War, Presidents and Public Opinion* (New York: Wiley, 1973).

20. Richard Nixon, *The Real War* (New York: Warner Books, 1980), p. 250.

5 | Evaluating the Carter Presidency

Presidential openness is not, of course, a new concept.[1] The "open presidency" is a code word for presidential behavior that pushes images of candor, disclosure, truthfulness, and access to the president by the people. The open presidency's rhetoric becomes the personalized rhetoric of a "people's" presidency which stresses the illusion that the president is a common man. Some presidents are mythologized into being great tellers of truths, such as George Washington, who presumably "never told a lie," or Abraham "Honest Abe" Lincoln. Other presidents are mythologized as being from the people, such as Andrew Jackson or Harry Truman. Indeed, Truman's myth grew large in 1974 during the post-Watergate fallout when he was celebrated for being a common and honest president, which was not quite the way his Republican opposition remembered it during 1945–53. Even Richard Nixon proclaimed his administration in 1969 to be the start of a new "open presidency."

Yet when Jimmy Carter came to the presidency promising to "never tell a lie" and to restore the open presidency, he was operating in a vastly different presidential environment that called for a symbolic end to the "imperial presidency." Largely, Carter's new presidential environment was determined by the impact that two important crises had on the American presidency—Vietnam and Watergate.

POST-WATERGATE PRESIDENCY

If Vietnam and Watergate altered relationships between citizens and their president in terms of trust and respect, and there appears to be abundant evidence that it did,[2] Vietnam and Watergate did not drastically alter the dynamics of the situation that led to the runaway-strong presidency. The forces that created the so-called imperial presidency are still operative, and, most important, Congress has not taken any adequate institutional responses to see that the situations do not develop again in the future. The War Powers Act is not a valid safeguard against unilateral presidential war making. Although it does appear to be a safeguard against a long drawn-out war without congressional approval, the president still has the ability to initiate action and to *inform*, rather than *consult*, Congress of his actions.

The Case Act requires the president and people who make agreements with foreign heads of state for the president to notify Congress of the agreements. The Case Act does not forbid the president to commit the United States unilaterally to foreign agreements via executive agreements. The Hughes-Ryan Amendment to the Foreign Assistance Act of 1974 requires that a president sign on to all covert operations and to inform the appropriate committees of Congress about the CIA covert operation. It does not offer sanctions for unreported or late reported covert operations undertaken by the president. Moreover, for the first time, Congress in the Hughes-Ryan Amendment admitted that in its view the president has the constitutional right to engage in unilateral covert operations.

The Supreme Court in *United States v. Nixon* (1974) appeared to hand down a decision that cut into the president's power when in a unanimous decision the Court ordered Nixon to turn over all relevant information and evidence needed for a criminal trial. But the Court ruled only that Nixon's particular claim to withhold the evidence was not valid; the Court did not strike down the notion of executive privilege. In fact, the Court for the first time admitted that presidents do have the right to make legitimate and valid requests to withhold certain kinds of information from Congress and the courts, namely national security secrets, in the name of executive privilege.[3]

About the only changes that resulted directly from Watergate were the Federal Election Campaign Act of 1974 and a professional code of ethics legislation for federal employees in 1976. Although the first reform seemed like a drastic change because it limited individual and group contributions in federal elections, strengthened reporting requirements, limited campaign spending, and allowed some public financing of presidential elections, the reform did not really change the relationship between money, power, and politics in this country. The legislation concerning a code of ethics for federal employees was not a serious safeguard against any future Watergates. This legislation was mainly used to investigate the false charges that Carter chief of staff Hamilton Jordan had once used cocaine at Studio 54 in New York.

Both post-Watergate presidents Ford and Carter argued that in foreign affairs Congress had tied the president's hands behind his back. They both argued that the War Powers Act and Hughes-Ryan Amendment were too restrictive. Moreover, both Ford and Carter called upon the House and Senate not to limit their options for covert responses.

Yet the country, or at least some observers, did seem to articulate some lessons that were "learned" throughout the Vietnam-Watergate eras, although there is no consensus on the "lessons" to be sure. James Thomson in his classic article "How Could Vietnam Happen?" in 1968 listed eighteen reasons why Vietnam happened:

1. Legacy of the 1950s-monolithic communism and the domino theory
2. Lack of Indochina expertise
3. The shadow of the loss of China
4. Domestication of dissenters
5. Preoccupation with Vietnam public relations as opposed to Vietnam policy making
6. Executive fatigue
7. Confusion as to what type of war we were fighting
8. Confusion as to how to end the war
9. Wishful thinking
10. Crypto-racism
11. Rhetorical escalation and problem of oversell

12. Posed fundamental test of U.S. will

13. Human ego investment

14. Persistent and repeated miscalculations

15. Steady give-in to pressures for a military solution

16. Missed opportunities to engage troops to leave

17. Abuse and distortion of history

18. The rise of a new breed of American ideologues who see Vietnam as the ultimate test of their doctrine.[4]

Moreover, Irving Janis suggested the reason that Vietnam was such a classic foreign policy fiasco was that the decision making with respect to Vietnam was colored by "groupthink."[5]

Beyond these reasons for failure in Vietnam, other observers noted lessons learned about the consequences of that failure. Ole Holsti and James Rosenau conducted research on "Vietnam, Consensus, and the Belief Systems of American Leaders" and found that the most important consequences learned by a wide range of elites from past supporters of Vietnam policy to critics of Vietnam policy included: among supporters (1) that Communists will seek other triumphs, (2) that American credibility had been damaged, (3) that the United States will limit its conception of the "national interest"; among critics (1) that long-term threats to the United States were neglected at the expense of Vietnam, (2) that faith was lost in the U.S. government, (3) that the U.S. economy was damaged as a result of U.S. participation, (4) that the United States will limit its conception of national interest, and (5) that American credibility was damaged.[6] Finally, with respect to ultimate lessons learned from Vietnam by supporters and critics, Holsti and Rosenau ranked in order the lessons learned by each group. For supporters of the Vietnam war, they learned:

1. Avoid graduated escalation

2. USSR is expansionist

3. Must honor alliance commitments

4. Domino theory is valid

5. Avoid half-measures militarily

6. Executive-congressional cooperation is vital

7. Americans do not understand role of power

8. Soviets abuse detente

9. Americans lack patience

10. Americans can't fight a limited war

11. Strike at the heart of enemy power

12. Communist victory is the antithesis of U.S. interest.

Critics of the war learned:

1. Avoid Angola involvement

2. Press is more likely to tell the truth on foreign policy

3. Excessive reliance on military advice

4. Rely too much on president to define the national interest

5. Third World revolutionaries are nationalistic

6. Scale down U.S. international role

7. Enlist UN cooperation.[7]

The many reasons for failure in Vietnam, the consequences of Vietnam, and the "lessons" learned from Vietnam all create part of the environment with which a U.S. president must deal in his foreign policy responsibilities.

The lessons from Watergate were less clear. American presidents could have learned that Nixon's failure can best be understood as staff failures and problems in organizing the presidency,[8] that Watergates have happened before and Nixon just got caught,[9] and that the system needs more restraints on presidential power or the system needs fewer restraints on presidential power, since Nixon's failure was the failure of a weak presidency.[10] However, it is not clear what lessons the American people actually selected about Watergate.

After Nixon's presidential performance in his open presidency (1969–74), new aspirants to the office were all forced to pay lip service to the open presidency. However, as Jimmy Carter noted, "Any candidate who personally professes to be honest immediately reminds the listeners of the pious pronouncements and protestations of our convicted former leaders."[11] Mere claims to an open presidency would not be enough to restore trust. For Carter, the problem of restoring trust in government was simple as indicated by his dictate, "There is a simple and effective way for public officials to regain public trust—be trustworthy."[12] In most democratic polities the notion of accountability is firmly grounded in the fragile concept of trust. Secrecy, lying, and deception are the antithesis of the open presidency and in order to establish an open presidency a president must minimize secret presidential behavior within the institutionalized presidential secrecy system.

Jimmy Carter's conception of the open presidency not only consists of the dimensions of presidential openness but also includes the dimensions of honesty, decency, and compassion.[13] Presidential openness is meaningless to Carter unless it is accompanied by the other images. On the campaign trail Carter emphasized that the first step in building an open presidency would consist of "stripping away secrecy."[14] The next step would be to establish honesty, decency, fairness, compassion, and openness within the presidency by presidential behavior and example. Yet Carter realized that dimensions of openness, decency, honesty, fairness, and compassion are not substantive. The evaluation of one's honesty and openness, for example, is inherently a relative and subjective determination. For Carter to succeed in establishing his dimensions within the open presidency he would have to at least establish the *appearance* of honesty, openness, compassion, fairness, and decency. This can be done most readily through the manipulation of political symbols, as Carter demonstrated during his administration.

On the campaign trail candidate Carter called for specific action in certain areas to help establish an open presidency. Among these steps were:

Politicians who seek to further their political careers through appeals to fears and prejudices must be exposed and rejected.

All-inclusive sunshine laws must be passed so that special interests will not retain their exclusive access behind closed government doors.

No gifts of value should ever again be permitted to a public official.

Complete revelation of all business and financial involvements of major officials should be required and none should be continued which constitute a possible conflict of interest.

Regulatory agencies must not be managed by representatives of the industry being regulated.

Public financing of campaigns should be extended to members of Congress.

Activities of lobbyists must be more thoroughly revealed and controlled.

Minimum secrecy within government should be matched with maximum personal privacy for citizens.

All federal judges, diplomats, and other major officials should be selected on the basis of merit.

Every effort should be extended to encourage full participation by our people in their government's processes, including universal voter registration for elections.

We must insure better public understanding of executive policy and better exchange of ideas between the Congress and the White House. To do this cabinet members representing the president should meet in scheduled and televised public interrogation sessions with the full bodies of Congress.[15]

These steps would provide the basis for an open presidency which would restore faith and confidence in the presidency, according to Carter. His list of steps contained the usual rhetoric about openness and honesty that most politicans employed, but Carter delivered the lines with a sense of urgency and with an incomparable moral tone. Few doubted Carter's sincerity, but many doubted Carter's ability to keep his promises once in office. Still others questioned whether Carter's concern with the process of the presidency was matched by his competency in the substantive areas of presidential programs and policies. An open presidency that does not solve problems or offer imaginative alternatives is a feeble presidency at best.

Carter's open presidency as revealed in the early days of his administration can be broken down into five analytical parts: his character, his style of managing, his position on disclosure/secrecy dilemma in a democracy, his early performance and job ratings, and his symbolic leadership.

Carter's presidential character appears beyond reproach. If Richard Neustadt's *Presidential Power* provided academic guidance for John Kennedy's presidency, then James Barber's *The Presidential Char-*

acter provided Carter with his academic guide.[16] Carter read Barber's work and he was impressed with it so much that he managed to meet with Barber to discuss the book. Carter classified himself as an "active-positive" in the Barber typology of presidential character, a classification that matches with great presidents like Franklin D. Roosevelt. Carter as the church-going, God-fearing, born-again Christian was strong on the intangible qualities needed to build presidential myth. Some called him a "southern-fried Kennedy" and some called him "Trumanesque." His folklike quality, character, and charisma were celebrated by his most ardent supporters. He had a special "manner of the man beneath the trappings of the office."[17] As Clinton Rossiter noted in his criteria for presidential greatness:

We remember a President as much for his quirks and quips as for his deeds and decisions. If he is not the sort of man around whose person legends will arise in profusion, he will surely not meet the final test of presidential greatness: to be enshrined as a folk hero in the American consciousness.[18]

Carter and the Carter-family myth were well on their way to become enshrined as original American folk-heroes, if they could deliver *substance.*

Carter's managerial style in the open presidency reflected an extraordinary concern for procedures over politics, according to Jack Knott and Aaron Wildavksy. In the first major article within the discipline on Carter's theory of governing, Knott and Wildavsky argued that Carter was an ideologue on governmental procedures—"procedures about which he speaks with passion, determination, and consistency."[19] Carter's concern was "less with particular goals than with the need for goals, less with the context of policies than with their ideal form—simplicity, uniformity, predictability, hierarchy, and comprehensiveness."[20] Knott and Wildavsky argued that Carter was concerned about how government apears to the people since appearance is a prerequisite for obtaining support to undertake action and policy. The open presidency must be conducted in a procedurally open fashion that stresses access to decision makers. Knott and Wildavsky felt that Carter would be inflexible on procedure and that his set of principles for managing the presidency were irrational for the pluralistic society of competing interests. They believed that Carter would take his case directly to the people if his procedural prescriptions for the open presidency were denied by Congress or special interests. In short, Carter would become "He-the-people" to interpret his victory and the people's victory for procedures.[21]

Carter's early position in the disclosure/secrecy dilemma within the democratic political system was suspect, but this was a function of the institutionalized presidential secrecy system rather than any great shortcoming on Carter's part. On the campaign trail candidate Carter called for an end to secrecy that pervaded the presidency. He attacked wrongdoing by the intelligence community and he condemned Henry Kissinger's secret diplomacy. Carter promised an open foreign policy with high moral standards. He assured the nation that he would never engage in any illegal, immoral, unethical, or unconstitutional actions within the intelligence communities. A new spirit of openness and high morality was promised in the foreign policy arena and in a *Playboy* interview during the transition, Hamilton Jordan said, "If, after the inauguration, you find a Cy Vance as Secretary of State and a Zbigniew Brzezinski as head of national security, then I would say we failed."[22]

To gain control of the Central Intelligence Agency once again, Carter nominated an outsider with the highest standards of moral integrity, Theodore Sorensen. When the political opposition from various special interests began to coalesce around the bogus charge that Sorensen leaked classified information and that he lacked respect for secrets, Sorensen's nomination appeared to be in trouble. Rather than put the full power of the presidency behind Sorensen's nomination and rather than staking out a clear contest between the Senate and the president, which Carter probably would have won, Carter stood behind his nomination in name only. Sorensen, sensing an unfavorable outcome without some genuine Carter arm-twisting, withdrew his nomination and the Carter administration lost a great friend of disclosure in the disclosure/secrecy dilemma. Carter more than compromised when he then nominated a military man, Admiral Stansfield Turner to be director of Central Intelligence. Turner called for criminal sanctions for agency employees and former employees who violated an oath of secrecy by disclosing secret information, and he told the

Senate Intelligence Committee that he would "certainly be amenable" to helping draft legislation for the Congress to provide for such sanctions.[23]

In another setback for the open presidency, Carter acted like some of his predecessors in defending covert operations and denouncing the leak of such operations which could harm the national security in his news conference on February 23, 1977. Carter was reacting to Bob Woodward's *Washington Post* story on the "payments" made by the CIA to King Hussein of Jordan and to other leaders. The Carter administration had tried to persuade Ben Bradlee and Bob Woodward not to go with the story, but Carter's personal "powers to persuade" were not convincing. The first White House response to the story came in the form of an uncharacteristic "no comment" from press secretary Jody Powell. Later at the news conference CBS reporter Bob Schieffer asked Carter:

In the last few days the White House issued "NO COMMENT" on the King Hussein–CIA secret payments. I asked Jody Powell if this had been revealed during the campaign would you have answered "NO COMMENT," then and Mr. Powell said, "I don't know." I wonder, Mr. President what would you have done?

President Carter: I don't know. (Laughter—on to the next question)

Within a week of the press conference Secretary of State Cyrus Vance publicly defended the practice of secretly sending funds to foreign leaders for spy operations, and Carter called for a cut in the access to presidential secrets. Carter wanted a single "very small" congressional oversight committee to have access to U.S. intelligence information rather than the present House and Senate intelligence committees. Later CIA director Turner called for more criminal sanctions against leakers when he said, "What we need is that there be some effective sanction to prevent the release of sensitive information."[24] Carter, in an effort to remind those who had by now forgotten where the president stood in regard to presidential openness, claimed that he favored minimizing the use of criminal penalties against leakers of classified information.

In some areas Carter's early performance and job ratings had been quite successful in the open presidency. On the campaign stops Carter had promised that one of his first acts as the president would be to grant amnesty for draft evaders of the Vietnam war. Two days after inauguration, Carter issued his amnesty proclamation. Carter said he would speak out for human rights in the international arena, but few expected Carter to be so sincere in his efforts. As president, Carter pushed the human rights theme in his foreign policy statements to the Soviet Union, Uganda, and other repressive regimes. UN ambassador Andrew Young also pushed the human rights issue at the United Nations. Carter pushed for procedural reforms to bring the presidency and the electoral process closer to the people and to make it more democratic. Critics claimed Carter was more interested in making the system favor Democrats when Carter proposed the abolition of the electoral college for direct popular vote, public financing of congressional elections, and voter registration on voting day. Yet these reforms proposed by Carter were in keeping with Carter's concerns for the procedurally open government. However, they had no chance for passage.

Carter scored other successes in easing the gap between the president and young people aged fifteen to twenty-five years when he became the first president to push for decriminalization for marijuana possession. As candidate Carter, he said the decriminalization of marijuana should be determined on a state-by-state basis since it was not a federal concern. As President Carter, he quickly moved to seek federal legislation that would decriminalize marijuana. Here was a president that had been supported by *Rolling Stone* magazine, Hunter S. Thompson (that symbol of gonzo journalism), and Phil Walden of Capricorn Records. Here was a president whose son had received a less than honorable discharge from the service for smoking marijuana. Carter was a president who enjoyed Southern rock music such as the Charlie Daniels Band, the Marshall Tucker Band, and the Allman Brothers Band. Carter especially liked Bob Dylan and once had Dylan stay at the governor's mansion in Georgia after a concert. In the 1960s many young people quoted Bob Dylan and demanded the legalization of marijuana. Ironically in 1977 it was the president of the United States who was quoting Dylan and asking for the decriminalization of marijuana. Again, this had no chance for passage.

The early Gallup results and the *Time* magazine poll published in March 1977 indicated that Carter's personal, open approach to the presidency was winning converts. Carter's popularity and job approval scores zoomed into the 70 percent level and the heady numbers represented a large margin which had been gained after his narrow victory over Ford in the November election. Yet much of the gain can probably be attributed to the vast reservoir of support that any president can expect during the first few months of his administration. However, the gain in popularity may also be attributed in part to Carter's huge success in his early symbolic leadership. By far, Carter's most successful presidential actions were on the symbolic level. His early symbolic performance was carried out like a virtuoso.

SYMBOLIC LEADERSHIP IN THE OPEN PRESIDENCY

In 1960 Daniel Boorstin detailed an important change in American life that reflected a shift in American thinking from talk about "ideals" to talk about "images." In his classic work *The Image: A Guide to Pseudo-Events in America* Boorstin argued that Americans had a passion for pseudoevents, synthetic heroes, prefabricated tourist attractions, and homogenized interchangeable forms of art and literature.[25] He argued that American life had become a showcase for images and pseudoevents.

Presidential press conferences fit into American pseudoevents and the institutionalized bureaucratic leak often serves as an ambiguous form of communication. Events are packaged and experience is blurred. Once the president becomes a celebrity, then it forces the citizen to deal with images and pseudoevents. Public opinion polls then tell citizens what it is thay they are already "thinking" about a person or an issue, as if citizens did not already know. Public opinion acts as a pseudoevent because it is forced into existence for the sole purpose of being reported.

Pseudoevents, such as presidential debates, are events that a political candidate stages in order to sell or promote his image. The pseudoevent possesses the following characteristics, according to Boorstin:

1. It is not spontaneous, but comes about because someone has planned, planted, or incited it. Typically, it is not a train wreck or an earthquake but an interview.

2. It is planted primarily (not always exclusively) for the immediate purpose of being reported or reproduced. Therefore, its occurrence is arranged for the convenience of the reporting or reproducing media. Its success is measured by how widely it is reported.

3. Its relation to the underlying reality of the situation is ambiguous.

4. Usually it is intended to be a self-fulfilling prophecy. The hotel's thirtieth-anniversary celebration, by saying that the hotel is a distinguished institution, actually makes it one.[26]

Moreover, pseudoevents overshadow spontaneous events in the following ways:

5. Pseudoevents are more dramatic.

6. Pseudoevents, being planned for dissemination, are easier to disseminate and to make vivid.

7. Pseudoevents can be repeated at will, and thus their impression can be reenforced.

8. Pseudoevents cost money to create; hence somebody has an interest in disseminating, magnifying, advertising, and extolling them as events worth watching or worth believing. They are therefore advertised in advance, and rerun in order to get money's worth.

9. Pseudoevents, being planned for intelligibility, are more intelligible and hence more reassuring.

10. Pseudoevents are more sociable, more conversable, and more convenient to witness.

11. Knowledge of pseudoevents—of what has been reported, or what has been staged, and how—becomes the test of being "informed."

12. Finally pseudoevents spawn other pseudoevents in geometric progression. They dominate our consciousness simply because there are more of them and ever more.[27]

As Boorstin has observed, pseudoevents have little to do with actually being able to govern.[28]

Candidates readily entered into the pseudoevents with similar goals in mind. Each candidate wanted to advertise his campagin in order to

1. solidify his support

2. attract the undecided vote

3. weaken opponent's support

4. share differences over substantive positions

5. highlight differences in personality, style, and image

6. increase turnout

7. be declared the winner by the appropriate opinion leaders

8. afford the opportunity to his opponent to embarrass himself.

In sum, most of the candidates' goals centered around "winning" the pseudoevents in order to win the election. The debates would only be useful if they had some electoral payoff for a candidate. Clearly, beyond the gains made by the mere participation in the debates, the challenge to each candidate was to win the debate. Since debates have many direct and indirect effects in the democratic process, the winning situation can be defined in many subtle ways for a pseudoevent.[29] One can win a debate if the major polls and opinion leaders declare one candidate to be the winner. If a majority of viewers clearly believe that one candidate gave a superior performance over the other candidate, "winners" are declared in the mass media. As Boorstin noted tongue-in-cheek, "How comforting to have some political matter we can grasp!"[30]

Jimmy Carter had a flair for political symbols. Indeed, political cartoonist G. B. Trudeau was moved to create a new character in his popular "Doonesbury" strip named Mr. Delecourt—the first "Secretary of Symbolism" in the Carter administration. Carter kicked off his 1976 presidential campaign from Warm Springs, Georgia— Franklin Roosevelt's home for his "Little White House," and the constant stream of political symbols gushed forth from the Carter camp. Carter evoked the names of Franklin Roosevelt, Harry Truman, and John Kennedy in his Warm Springs speech as two Roosevelt sons stood with Carter. The stream of political symbols evoked to build the Carter image never stopped.

The Georgia "peanut farmer" had been good copy throughout the entire 1976 presidential campaign. He was religious and from the South. He was a small farmer with a remarkable family that included "Miss Lillian," Rosalynn, Amy, a faith healer, and "Brother Billy" among others. He had the great smile and set of teeth in which cartoonists delighted. Comedians easily learned how to do the Carter accent as he became a political celebrity, but, most important, he seemed to be winning primaries.

Carter photographed well and he was very comfortable under questioning by newspeople. Although the speeches were basically from the same stock speech, Carter had his positions and answers down very well. When Bill Moyers asked Carter to define politics, he had an answer which surprised even Moyers. Carter did not define politics as "conflict management," "the art of the possible," "everything," Lasswell's "who gets what, when, and how," or David Easton's "the authoritative allocation of values for a society." Carter defined politics as "the pursuit of justice in a sinful world," from Reinhold Niebuhr's work.

In his inaugural address Carter presented a simple and humble message. He asked the nation in the words of the prophet Micah to renew the search for humility, mercy, and justice. Carter said: "You have given me a great responsibility to stay close to you, to be worthy of you, and to exemplify what you are. Let us create together a new national spirit of unity and trust. Your strength can compensate for my weakness, and your wisdom can help minimize my mistakes."[31] The speech contained no passionate lines like John Kennedy's inaugural address, but Carter delivered it with his usual sincerity and dedication. Afterward, Carter began delivering on his promise to institute an open presidency, at least in the symbolic sense, when he and his wife walked to the inaugural stand for the parade. This gesture was the first of many inventive symbolic moves that characterized the Carter administration.

Carter conducted fireside chats on national television and he conducted the first national presidential phone-in show along with Walter Cronkite, which received glowing reviews from most critics. Carter attended a town meeting in Massachusetts and slept with an "average" American family. He cut back on some perquisites for White House staff and he minimized the playing of the song "Hail to the Chief." All of these symbolic acts had the effect of showing that the president was a humble, common man who wanted to make every effort possible to stay close to the American people and to find out what was on their minds. In short, it was a rather remarkable public relations effort in which Carter was trying to expand his base of public support. His early efforts appeared to have been successful in the short run.

Yet the early days of the Carter presidency also showed that the fundamental desire of the president to control national secrets within his "open presidency" would still remain. Although Carter engaged in some "open" gestures, he was essentially trying to keep the same institutionalized presidential secrecy system intact which operated under Johnson, Nixon, and even Ford.

The new Carter administration made it clear that the past abuses committed by the intelligence community in the name of national security would not occur during the Carter presidency. Vice-President Mondale thought that former President Ford and the director of the CIA under Ford, George Bush, had done a good job in bringing the CIA under control. He noted that the CIA under Ford did not attempt any assassination plots or any paramilitary operations, and thus some honor had been restored to the CIA before Carter took over.[32] The new director of the CIA under Carter, Stansfield Turner, told the Senate Intelligence Committee that he would authorize disclosure of the lump sum that the intelligence agencies spent each year.[33] Turner also fired two agents who performed "unauthorized" favors for friends by supplying them with bomb detonators which were to be sold to Libya.[34] Turner made the scandal public in an effort to show that he had control over the agency in terms of questionable activities.

Carter's "open presidency" had to operate under new institutional relationships with the Senate because the Select Committee on Intelligence became a permanent committee on May 19, 1976.[35] The committee has the power to release classified intelligence information over the objection of a president if it follows specified procedures. If eight or more members of the fifteen-person committee want to make some CIA information public, they can bring the matter to the whole Senate for a vote in secret session. If the Senate votes to release the classified material, it will be released. If any person releases the classified information prior to a vote by the Senate, that person would be subject to disciplinary action according to Senate Resolution 400 which created the permanent committee. If the violator is a member of the Senate, that person could be subject to censure or expulsion, and if the violator is a staff member, the person would be subject to a citation for contempt or termination of employment.

Within the first eight months of his administration Carter had proposed new secrecy rules by circulating a draft of an executive order that would take classification authority away from ten government agencies and limit the authority for others.[36] Yet critics charged that Carter was no more open than Gerald Ford. Former Secretary of State Henry Kissinger claimed that Carter was conducting "secret diplomacy" just like the diplomacy Carter had criticized Kissinger for using during the 1976 presidential campaign. Kissinger said, "[Carter and Vance] may find it painful to admit this but secret diplomacy is unavoidable."[37]

It was still quite evident during the Carter administration's first months that the control of national security secrets would remain within the presidential secrecy system. In April 1977 the Justice Department successfully prosecuted a college student on espionage and conspiracy charges for passing secrets to the Soviet Union.[38] About six months later, however, the presidential secrecy system demonstrated that it could declassify information whenever it so desired when Secretary of Defense Harold Brown told reporters that U.S. intelligence analysts had learned that the Soviets had developed a weapon that could attack U.S. space satellites.[39] The Carter administration could have withheld that information but chose to publicize it in order to let the Soviets know that the United States had knowledge of their weapon and possibly to create support within Congress for appropriations for a similar U.S. weapon. Presumably, if an American citizen had made the same announcement that Secretary of Defense Brown had made to reporters, that citizen might have been considered to have leaked classified information. As Jody Powell, the president's press secretary noted, the underlying operating principle in the whole secrecy/disclosure dilemma was still simply, "Trust me, folks."[40]

THE FAILURE OF THE CARTER PRESIDENCY

After Carter's original media successes that came out of his early succession of presidential pseudoevents, the central question remained regarding Carter's conduct of the symbolically open president; that is, at what point does lack of substantive achievement undermine symbolic success? Carter had to deliver in the substantive areas of meaningful programs and policies which would be addressed to meet the needs of various groups within the electorate and the public.

The answer to the central question became clear by the end of the first year of the Carter presidency. By late 1977 and well into 1978, presidential watchers and public opinion leaders started asking nagging questions about Carter's ability to handle the job of president. The Bert Lance affair began to tarnish the image of Carter as a different kind of trustworthy president. It appeared that Carter also could have members of his administration involved in public scandals. The major press, all in "rat-pack" fashion,[41] began to question Carter's competency, as if the presidency were a job that had competency-based tests before one took office. The conventional wisdom was that Democratic President Carter could not get his legislative programs through the Democratic-controlled House and Senate. Carter was charged as being the outsider who did not know how to stroke the appropriate members of Congress like Speaker Tip O'Neill. The empirical evidence did not support this charge, but since most opinion leaders believed that Carter could not deal with Congress, this image persisted. George Edwards has shown that Carter's presidential influence in Congress actually was comparable with the so-called model of strong presidential legislative leadership, Lyndon Johnson. In Carter's first two years he received presidential victories on congressional votes on which he took a clear position over 75 percent of the time.[42] Moreover, in 1978 Carter scored presidential victories 85 percent of the time in the Senate, a score that one has to go back to Lyndon Johnson's record in 1965 to top.[43]

The problem with the Carter administration during 1977 and 1978 was an inability to use public relations to receive credit for presidential victories. Even though Carter showed promise as a manipulator of symbols with respect to honesty, openness, trust, and compassion, the administration was unable to project an image of Carter as a *competent* president. Carter was attacked by many because of inflation, unemployment, and the energy crisis, as if he was single-handedly responsible for the state of the American economy. Carter proposed major changes but Congress did not "dispose" in the words of former Speaker Sam Rayburn. Congress was asserting a newfound independence and special interests dominated most the the legislative output. Congress continued to take a stronger role in foreign policy matters and the president found it difficult to control or even to persuade members of his own party to support some of his legislative programs. The Democrats in Congress were less cohesive, less disciplined, and less inclined toward party responsibility than other Congresses that faced Democratic presidents. Thus, Carter's relatively strong legislative record with respect to presidential victories is even more impressive.

As James Wooten noted, even when Carter scored what was termed a victory for the president, the media often played up aspects other than presidential competency. When the Senate ratified the complex and controversial Panama Canal Treaty, Wooten noted that "much of the public relations triumph went to 'courageous' Senators rather than to the Carter team that had principally steered the treaties through."[44]

Given the perception that Carter was incompetent, inept, and unable to deal with the problems confronting America, the administration in 1978 realized its inability to sell Carter victories and programs. The administration brought back to the Carter staff media advisor and public relations expert Gerald Rafshoon. Rafshoon had played a crucial role in the rise of Jimmy Carter in the 1976 campaign and it was hoped that he could perform a similar miracle with Carter's image.

Indeed, by the end of 1978 Carter's image seemed to be on the rebound. He was generally given outstanding marks for his formal recognition of China and his Camp David Summit work to bring Anwar Sadat and Menachem Begin together.

Yet Rafshoon was unable to work symbolic miracles with respect to the president's image and the economy. The long gasoline lines, irate consumers, OPEC price hikes, and major oil companies' profits in the summer of 1979 were all cited as examples of Carter's inability to solve problems. Carter was scored for not providing "leadership." By October 1979 the Carter presidency was in shambles. Senator Ted Kennedy held substantial leads over Carter in all the major polls and Carter's popularity had fallen during the economic crisis in 1979 to the lowest level of public support ever recorded for a president, even lower than Richard Nixon's final Watergate days.

Then in November 1979 Iranian militants took over the American embassy in Teheran, Iran, and held the American citizens hos-

tage after Carter had let the Shah of Iran into the country for med-
ical treatment. Carter was able to define this event as a "crisis" for
the public. By manipulating the symbol of the president in crisis,
Carter was able to begin to turn his public opinion scores upward.
Later in 1979 when the Soviet Union invaded Afghanistan, the
Carter administration was able to use this as a threat to national
security. By using Iran and the events in Afghanistan as major foreign policy crises, Carter was able to project the image of the president in "action." Kennedy's opposition on the campaign trail was
essentially quieted with respect to foreign policy as the President
adopted a "rose garden strategy," à la Gerald Ford in 1976 and
Richard Nixon in 1972, of being too busy being president to have
time to campaign for the presidency.

Of course Carter's strategy worked in the short run as Kennedy's
campaign failed to capture support due to the president's national
security uplift, Kennedy's uneven campaigning, and the revival of
the political symbol "Chappaquiddick." Carter revived the rhetoric
of the Cold War and asked citizens to support an Olympic boycott,
a grain embargo, and other measures designed to stand up to the
Soviets. With respect to the Iranian situation, the president condemned Iran in the international arena of public opinion, urged
diplomacy as the only means to resolve the crisis, and froze Iranian
assets within the United States. Democrats rallied behind the incumbent president and Carter was assured the 1980 Democratic
nomination because of preconvention strategy to garner as many
delegates as possible and to win most of them in the primaries.

The Carter image comeback was successful only within the activist groups in the Democratic party, because after Carter was re-
nominated in the summer of 1980 his small lead in the polls over
Republican challenger Ronald Reagan began to reverse itself. Reagan was able to manipulate countersymbols to the symbolic blitz
by the president to force many in the electorate to focus on Carter's economic record. Moreover, Reagan was able to turn Carter's
short-run successes in the foreign policy crises of Iran and Afghanistan into symbols of Carter's overall weakness and impotence in
foreign policy. The long-term impact of Carter's decision to label
Afghanistan and Iran as crises finally came back to haunt the president in his role as symbol manipulator. Within every attempt to
manipulate symbols for the public, all presidents must realize that

symbolic victories must be accompanied by tangible victories in order to show the public that under the symbol some substance does exist. Carter failed to deliver on his claim that the Iranian situation and the Soviet invasion of Afghanistan were strong security threats since he was unable to secure the release of the hostages before the election and since he was unable to force the Soviet troops out of Afghanistan.

By election time, Carter was unable to convince a majority of voters that Reagan was a "trigger-happy" warmonger and thus Carter had to stand or fall on his own record. With rampant inflation, high levels of unemployment, extremely high interest rates, and unstable energy sources, Carter had to defend an economic record that was indefensible in terms of the partisan rhetoric of the campaign. Moreover, Carter had to deal with a series of unfulfilled promises dating back to his 1976 campaign rhetoric, such as his promises to balance the federal budget and to cut down the federal bureaucracy. Finally, the hostage situation in Iran had reached unprecedented symbolic levels in the minds of most Americans due to the excessive media coverage, and Carter had not been able to solve the situation that he had labeled a crisis.

Given this campaign record, in retrospect it is probably still a wonder that the Democratic party nominated its incumbent president. But hindsight is perfect sight. Reagan defeated Carter in an electoral college landslide and he also scored an impressive victory in the popular vote. Perhaps Carter's greatest victory came near the end of his presidency when he successfully negotiated the release of the American hostages as the Reagan administration was coming to power on January 20, 1981.

PRESIDENTIAL RESPONSES TO HOSTAGE CRISES

For the president who is trying to live up to the image of the macho presidential style, the "crisis" situation gives the president the opportunity to make decisions to attempt to manage events. Moreover, the president is given an opportunity to appear in control of his emotions, to appear "cool under fire," and to appear like a macho decision maker.

Since 1968 American presidents have had three key opportunities to react to hostage crises situations. President Lyndon Johnson had the *Pueblo* crisis of 1968 when North Korea captured a crew of eighty-three hostages, President Gerald Ford had the *Mayaguez* incident in 1975 when Cambodia captured a crew of forty men, and President Jimmy Carter had the Iranian hostage situation of 1979–81 when Iranian militants held fifty-three American hostages. Each of these situations presented different circumstances for the decision makers and each decision maker responded in a different fashion. President Johnson tried diplomatic solutions, President Ford tried military solutions, and President Carter tried both diplomatic and military solutions to get the return of the hostages. Each president was ultimately successful in gaining the release of the hostages, but each president was judged in different ways with respect to the handling of the crises.

Pueblo Incident

When gathering electronic intelligence off the coast of North Korea, the U.S. *Pueblo* was seized by North Korean patrol boats and a crew of eighty-three was taken hostage on January 24, 1968. Commander Lloyd Bucher's ship did not put up a struggle as the ship was escorted to the port of Wonsan. The North Korean government demanded that the U.S. government admit that the *Pueblo* was spying within North Korean waters less than twelve miles from the coast. President Lyndon Johnson refused to classify the *Pueblo* as a spy ship and the U.S. government claimed that the ship was in international waters.

Johnson decided not to treat the incident as a presidential crisis situation which required constant presidential attention. Johnson was bogged down with the war in Indochina, the fallout from the Tet offensive, the 1968 presidential election politics, and the domestic situation at home. Major networks did not cover the story from inside of North Korea and the public attention span was not totally focused on the incident. In other times, this act by North Korea would have been grounds for a declaration of war by the United States or for some swift military response. During the winter of 1968, the Johnson administration attempted to play down the incident and to engage in diplomacy to secure the release of the crew and the ship.

In order to secure the release of the crew, the Johnson administration had only to admit the spying charges were true. The Johnson administration decided this option would be too much of a humiliating situation for the government and the administration. Johnson's first response was typical of the macho presidential style. On January 25, 1968, the USS *Enterprise* and four destroyers took up positions off the coast of South Korea and the next day Johnson ordered 14,787 Air Force and Navy reservists to active duty. By January 28, 1968, South Korea had initiated a large-scale military buildup. North Korea's response to this military pressure was to threaten to put the crew on trial as spying criminals. Within one week of the capture, members of Congress and various commentators and opinion leaders had scored Commander Bucher for his failure to fight and had denounced the Johnson administration for letting this incident happen. Governor of California Ronald Reagan attacked Johnson for his failure to act immediately. He accused Johnson of continuing the policy of "appeasement."

The administration tried to get the USSR to pressure North Korea into releasing the crew and the United States tried to get UN action against North Korea. By February 3, North Korea had indicated that one crewman had died and that another crewman, Lieutenant Harris, had confessed to being a spy. The efforts to get the Soviet Union to play a mediating role failed and domestic politicians again began to attack the Johnson administration for failure to act.

However, one politician offered an unusual antimacho proposal to solve the situation. Republican front-runner for the presidential nomination Richard M. Nixon suggested on February 6, 1968, that the United States might consider apologizing to North Korea if it would secure the release of the crew. A Gallup poll of February 11, 1968, showed that only 40 percent of American respondents backed the use of force to get back the *Pueblo* and a Harris poll revealed that most Americans did not want to go to war over the issue.

North Korea demanded that the United States deescalate the situation in the area and announced that another crew member, Lieutenant Murphy, had confessed. The Johnson administration responded by warning against any attempts by North Korea to punish crewmen. In March, North Korea released the text of letters from crewmen to President Johnson urging the president to apologize to North Korea for spying in their waters and to promise that it would never happen again. North Korea produced five letters from crewmen to relatives, including a letter from Commander Bucher that admitted the espionage charges were true. The Johnson administration still refused to admit the spying by the *Pueblo* and the administration informed the Senate Foreign Relations Committee of its official version of events.

With Johnson's famous March 31, 1968, dovish speech about the war in Indochina where Johnson took himself out of running for reelection, the administration no longer acted as if the return of the *Pueblo* crew was an important calculation in terms of Johnson's election. Yet other presidential candidates continued to suggest solutions for the problem. Candidate Eugene McCarthy suggested on April 20, 1968, that the administration pay ransom to North Korea to get the crew back, but Secretary of State Dean Rusk quickly ruled out ransom. He also admitted that the negotiations were deadlocked. In May, candidate and Vice-President Hubert Humphrey suggested that the return of the *Pueblo* crew be placed on the negotiating table at the Paris Peace Talks to end the war in Vietnam. On May 23, 1968, Governor Reagan again attacked the Johnson administration for its failure to respond to the situation. He said the U.S. forces in the Pacific failed to help the *Pueblo* because they were equipped for the nuclear response only.

By July 16, 1968, Secretary of State Rusk refused to bow to interest group pressure from families of the captured crewmen to hurry up the release. One group, "Remember the *Pueblo* Committee," demanded that the United States set a deadline for the release of the crew, but Rusk declined to set a deadline. On July 27, 1968, a Japanese television film showed Commander Bucher writing a letter to President Johnson asking for a U.S. apology. Yet publicly the Johnson administration showed no signs of offering any apologies to North Korea.

By September 1968 a South Korean newspaper reported that the United States had secretly met with North Korea to discuss the contents of a letter of apology. On September 18, 1968, families of the crewmen of the *Pueblo* marched on the State Department but Secretary Rusk refused to meet with them. The families were demanding that the United States *not* apologize for the incident. Candidate Nixon stopped offering constructive suggestions for the release of the crew and on September 25, 1968, Nixon called the capture of ship and crew an "incredible humiliation for U.S."

The story of the *Pueblo* clearly had been treated as second-rate news throughout the presidential campaign of 1968. With Johnson out of the race, it was not deemed a productive tactic to criticize continually a lame duck administration in its efforts to save the lives of the crew. By November, with Richard Nixon's election to the presidency, it became clearer to North Korea that a Nixon administration would be tough in negotiating the release of the crew and the ship. After the November elections, the deadlocked talks with the Johnson administration and North Korean officials over the release of the crew suddenly became unthawed. Perhaps it was fear of Nixon or perhaps the Johnson administration wanted to end Johnson's unpopular presidency on a successful note, but the United States began softening its position. In December, some families of the hostage crew went to East Berlin to try to negotiate the release of their sons because they did not feel that the Johnson administration was doing enough to get the *Pueblo* crew home. However, the Johnson administration began to move quickly one week before Christmas.

On December 23, 1968, the United States signed a confession of espionage inside North Korean territorial waters. Once Johnson had done this, as North Korea had demanded, the entire crew of the *Pueblo* was released. Once the *Pueblo* crew crossed over into South Korea, the Johnson administration immediately repudiated the "confession" and admitted that it had lied in order to get the crew returned. Commander Bucher said his men were forced into signing confessions of spying and he said once again at his news conference that the *Pueblo* did not invade North Korean territorial waters.

In over eleven months of captivity, the negotiating position that would secure the release of the crew remained the same in the eyes of North Korea. It would simply take a U.S. admission of guilt and the crew would be set free. It took the Johnson administration almost a year to come up with its unusual idea of admitting guilt and on the same day of denying the confession.[45]

Mayaguez Incident

The SS *Mayaguez*, a merchant ship from the United States, was attacked and seized by Cambodian naval forces on May 12, 1975. After meeting with the National Security Council some nine hours after the attack, President Gerald Ford issued a statement claiming that the attack was an act of "piracy" and that "failure by the Cambodians to release the ship would have the most serious consequences."[46]

In most decisive fashion, Ford opted for a macho presidential style solution—to send in the marines! After early diplomatic efforts appeared to fail in the eyes of the Ford administration, the president gave the orders to secure the ship and to liberate the crew. As a report by the comptroller general put it, there was a "perceived need for quick action."[47] The study observed:

One Defense official told us that Cambodia was believed to be acting to embarrass the United States and its prime motive was to gain control of American prisoners of war to use for various purposes . . . another Defense official told us that if the crew reached the Cambodian mainland, a diplomatic solution—similar to the negotiations to secure the release of the *Pueblo* crew—would have been about the only alternative.[48]

On May 14, 1975, the U.S. Marines attacked the Koh Tang island where the crew was believed to have been held. Another group of marines boarded the *Mayaguez* and found it had been abandoned. One hour after the assault on the island, the Ford administration realized that diplomatic efforts to release the ship had been successful and that Cambodia was about to release the ship. Since the president did not detect any mention of the crew in the Cambodian broadcast of concession, the rescue mission proceeded. During the rescue mission a total of forty-one soldiers lost their lives in order to save a forty-member crew. Eighteen marines died in combat and twenty-three members of a U.S. Air Force rescue crew died in a related Thailand crash. Of the eight helicopters used in the first wave assault on the island, three crashed and two were disabled. Moreover, the prolonged assault on the island by the marines was actually unnecessary since the crew was no longer being held on that island.

While the assault continued, Cambodia had already been prepared to release the entire crew in unharmed condition. In fact the crew was on a fishing vessel waving white flags to the USS *Wilson*. After the crew was safely returned to the *Wilson*, the operations to remove the marines safely from the island continued with more hostilities, and the Cambodian mainland was hit with a series of bombing raids to show Cambodia that the Ford administration really meant business.

This macho rescue attempt, which really did not liberate any hostages, was probably the finest moment in the Ford administration as perceived by most presidential watchers. Ford's popularity in public opinion polls jumped after the *Mayaguez* incident. He was portrayed as a decisive, unemotional, and manly presidential leader who took quick, bold action to save the United States from embarrassment. It was the United States' last show of force in Indochina, and the unnecessary bombing raids on the mainland and the quick trigger rescue decision made many citizens feel good again because their macho president had not let them down. Once again, the macho presidential style was very costly.

Iranian Hostage Crisis

On November 4, 1979, militant Iranian students took over the American embassy in Teheran. They demanded that the United States return Shah Pahlavi and his wealth to Iran in exchange for the hostages. The Carter administration refused to return the Shah of Iran to face punishment under the new regime in Iran headed by Ayatollah Khomeini. This continued the so-called Iranian hostage crisis.

The Carter administration immediately labeled the takeover of an American embassy as a crisis. The news media responded by playing up the incident as front-page news and as lead story on network newscasts. Indeed, the televised media presented a forum for the Iranian militants to denounce the United States and President Jimmy Carter. The coverage of the demonstrations became a ritual in which the major television networks became an unwitting participant for the anti-American propaganda of Iranian militants who shouted, "Death to the Shah, Death to America, Death to Carter." Network news shows started counting the number of days that the hostages had been in captivity and one network, ABC, started a late-night news program to update the hostage situation. This show later developed into ABC's "Nightline" with Ted Koppel.

If the president and the major networks call the takeover a crisis, then it becomes one. If the *Pueblo* incident had as much coverage in 1968 as the Iranian militant takeover in 1979, one wonders how this would have affected the outcome of the negotiations.

The Carter administration played partisan politics with the situation at first. It was time for the American people to rally around the president during this crisis, especially so for all those people who had the nerve to challenge the incumbent president for the Democratic party nomination. The Carter administration tried the diplomatic solution, but the students demands were inflexible. The Carter administration also tried to have its allies put pressure on the government of Iran to release the embassy workers. UN pressure and pressure from the International Court of Justice had no effect on releasing the hostages. The Carter administration wanted the return of the hostages before the United States would consider Iranian grievances about past U.S. support of the represive regime of the Shah. Under no circumstances would the United States trade the Shah for the hostages, according to the Carter administration.

Yet Carter had also been proceeding with a military rescue solution. By April 24, 1980, the Carter administration had decided to unleash its military rescue plan. With visions of the Israeli rescue at Entebbe, the Carter administration took a page out of the Gerald Ford book on hostage situations and sent in the U.S. marines. Again eight helicopters took off for a daring rescue mission much like the *Mayaguez* helicopter missions, and the result was a similar technological helicopter disaster. One helicopter went down after leaving the USS *Nimitz*, one lost its way in a dust storm and returned to the carrier, and one landed in the desert with an unfixable malfunction. This left five helicopters for a mission that needed six, so the mission had to be aborted. While leaving the mission site, one helicopter crashed into a tanker plane and eight soldiers lost their lives. The mission was a total failure.

The Carter administration then returned to negotiations with an effort to secure the release of the hostages and not to lose national honor. With the election of Ronald Reagan in November 1980, the negotiations began to get back on track presumably because the Iranian militants worried about what kind of rescue attempts the macho Reagan would attempt. The election of a hard-line Republican president with respect to foreign policy worked much like the 1968 election of Richard Nixon worked to unfreeze the negotiations for the release of the *Pueblo* crew from North Korea. Finally, after some 444 days of captivity, the Carter administration worked out a deal where the hostages would be released on the inaugural day of the new American president. Once again all the hostages were returned and no hostages were killed by their capturers.

Each of the hostage situations was different, yet they all called for American presidents to get the return of the hostages in unharmed condition and for the U.S. president not to embarrass the country. In the *Pueblo* case eight crew members died in the initial seizure, but the Johnson administration successfully got the return of eighty-two hostages after some eleven months of negotiating by using a brilliant tactic, that is, give in to the demands of the other side and then denounce the concessions and claim they were made under duress after the hostages are returned. The Ford administration opted for the macho presidential response of sending in the marines. As a result of the foolhardy mission, forty-one soldiers died in trying to save forty crew members who had been released. This fact hardly mattered to the American people and Ford's solution of using military force was widely greeted as the success story of his administration. Carter on the other hand appeared indecisive. He delayed his macho military response too long and when he finally tried the daring rescue mission, it was an absolute failure. The box score was eight marines killed in trying to rescue fifty-two hostages who were later returned unharmed, mainly because a tough, macho Republican president, Ronald Reagan, was elected to the American presidency and because of the Carter administration's tireless efforts to solve the crisis diplomatically.

Conclusions

The Carter administration was an administration that took a roller-coaster ride in the public opinion polls largely because of an inability to project a constant symbol of Carter's presidency. The

Carter image could successfully be projected in the short run but when substantive victories did not match the symbolic output of the administration, Carter's popularity suffered. Ironically, the failure of the Carter administration was that of a public relations failure. Image molders like Hamilton Jordan, Jody Powell, Robert Strauss, and Gerald Rafshoon forgot to sell the president's substantive achievements and programs with the same fervor that they tried to sell the Carter image.

Among the Carter successes that were undersold to the public included Carter's human rights program, the Latin American policy, the African policy, the lack of military interventionism, the Panama Canal Treaty, the Camp David Summit, the open presidency, and, finally, the brilliant diplomatic effort to get the hostages returned in safe and sound condition. Domestically, Carter was the first American president who tried to inform the American people about the problems of the finite supply of energy and resources. The messenger who brought the bad news was in effect beheaded in the court of public opinion. Carter had a strong record in protection of the environment and in civil service reform. He also championed in his rhetoric the needs of disadvantaged groups in American society such as women, blacks, Hispanics, and the hanicapped, while he scored a series of strong judicial appointments.

In short, Carter behaved like the traditional liberal Democratic president in his rhetoric while trying to govern as a moderate. He surely has to be labeled an "active-positive" in James Barber's terminology.[49] But as political scientists learned, this designation alone does not insure presidential greatness or "near-great" labels. Carter was the best example of symbolic manipulation of presidential symbols gone wild. Clearly his administration was unable to resolve the dissonance that resulted in a "feeble" presidency when citizens could not match symbolic output with reality. The key reason why citizens could not do this was because of the extraordinary negative press that Carter received throughout his presidency.

NOTES

1. See John Orman, *Presidential Secrecy and Deception: Beyond the Power to Persuade* (Westport, Conn.: Greenwood Press, 1980).

2. See Gallup poll data in *Every Four Years*, PBS television show and publication for January 1980. See also Arthur H. Miller, "Public Policy and Political Cynicism: 1964–1970," in Norman Luttbeg, ed., *Public Opinion and Public Policy*, rev. ed. (Homewood, Ill.: Dorsey Press, 1974); F. C. Arterton, "The Impact of Watergate on Childrens' Attitudes toward Political Authority," *Political Science Quarterly*, vol. 89 (June 1974); and see Orman, *Presidential Secrecy and Deception*.

3. *United States v. Nixon* (1974), 42 U.S.L.W. 5237, and see Theodore Sorensen, *Watchmen in the Night* (Cambridge, Mass.: MIT Press Paperback, 1976), pp. 120–21.

4. James Thomson, "How Could Vietnam Happen?" *Atlantic Monthly*, vol. 22, April 1968, pp. 47–53.

5. Irving Janis, "Escalation of the Vietnam War: How Could It Happen?" *Victims of Groupthink* (Boston: Houghton Mifflin, 1972), pp. 101–36.

6. Ole R. Holsti and James N. Rosenau, "Vietnam, Consensus, and the Belief Systems of American Leaders," *World Politics*, vol. 32, no. 1 (October 1979), p. 31.

7. Ibid., p. 50.

8. See Richard Johnson, *Managing the White House* (New York: Harper & Row, 1974); Dan Rather and Gary Gates, *The Palace Guard* (New York: Warner Books, 1975); Stephen Hess, *Organizing the Presidency* (Washington, D.C.: Brookings Institution, 1976); and Richard P. Nathan, *The Plot That Failed: Nixon and the Administrative Presidency* (New York: Wiley, 1975).

9. Victor Lasky, *It Didn't Start with Watergate* (New York: Dial Press, 1977).

10. See Charles Hardin, *Presidential Power and Accountability* (Chicago: University of Chicago Press, 1974), and the counterargument in Sorensen, *Watchmen in the Night*.

11. Jimmy Carter, *Why Not the Best?* (New York: Bantam Books, 1976), p. 168.

12. Ibid.

13. Ibid., p. 167.

14. Ibid., p. 168.

15. Ibid., pp. 168–70.

16. Richard Neustadt, *Presidential Power* (New York: Wiley, 1960), and James Barber, *The Presidential Character* (Englewood Cliffs, N.J.: Prentice-Hall, 1972).

17. Clinton Rossiter, *The American Presidency*, rev. ed. (New York: Mentor Books, 1962), p. 139.

18. Ibid.

19. Jack Knott and Aaron Wildavsky, "Jimmy Carter's Theory of Governing," *Wilson Quarterly* (Winter 1977), pp. 49–67.

20. Cited in David Broder, "The Principles Guiding Carter May Not Work in Government," *Louisville Courier-Journal*, February 13, 1977, p. D-3.

21. Knott and Wildavsky, "Jimmy Carter's Theory of Governing," p. 63.

22. Quoted in "Loose Talk," *Rolling Stone*, March 10, 1977, p. 39.

23. "CIA Nominee Wouldn't Allow Assassinations," AP wire story, *Louisville Courier-Journal*, February 23, 1977, p. A-5.

24. "Punishment for Leaking Secrets Studies," Washington Post–LA Times Service, *Louisville Courier-Journal*, March 10, 1977, p. A-4.

25. Daniel Boorstin, *The Image* (New York: Harper and Row, 1961), p. 39.

26. Ibid., pp. 39–40.

27. Ibid.

28. Ibid., p. 42.

29. Doris Graber, *Verbal Behavior and Politics* (Urbana: University of Illinois Press, 1976), pp. 229–33.

30. Boorstin, *The Image*, pp. 39–40.

31. "Text of Inaugural Address," *Indianapolis Star*, January 21, 1977, p. 10.

32. Walter Mondale, interview on February 22, 1977, on PBS's "McNeil/Lehrer Report."

33. "Lump Sum Budget Item OK Says CIA Boss," UPI story, *Indianapolis Star*, April 28, 1977, p. 8.

34. "CIA Director Fires Two Agents for Favors," UPI story, *Indianapolis Star*, April 28, 1977, p. 8.

35. John T. Elliff, "Congress and the Intelligence Community" in Lawrence Dodd, Bruce Oppenheimer, eds. *Congress Reconsidered*, (New York: Praeger, 1977), p. 203.

36. "Carter Plan Would Limit Top Secrets," AP story, *Indianapolis Star*, September 15, 1977, p. 1.

37. "Secret Diplomacy Conducted under Carter: Kissinger," UPI story, from *London Observer* interview by Douglas Rater and Kenneth Harris, in the *Indianapolis Star*, June 20, 1977, p. 3.

38. Linda Deutsch, "Jury Finds Student Guilty of Passing U.S. Secrets," AP story, *Louisville Courier-Journal*, April 29, 1977, p. A-8.

39. Fred S. Hoffman, "Defense Chief Says Russia Has Anti-Satellite Weapon," AP story, *Louisville Courier-Journal*, October 5, 1977, p. 1.

40. Jody Powell, quoted in "President's Boys," *Time*, June 6, 1977, p. 18.

41. Timothy Crouse, *The Boys on the Bus* (New York: Random House, 1973).

42. George Edwards, *Presidential Influence in Congress* (San Francisco: W. H. Freeman, 1980), pp. 19, 20.

43. Ibid., p. 19.

44. James Wooten, *Dasher* (New York: Warner Books, 1979), p. 373.

45. See *New York Times Index, 1968* (New York: The New York Times, 1969), pp. 732–736.

46. *Seizure of the Mayaguez,* part IV, Reports of the Comptroller General of the United States Submitted to the Subcommittee on International Political and Military Affairs of the House Committee on International Relations, October 4, 1976, p. 63.

47. Ibid., p. 71.

48. Ibid., p. 72.

49. James Barber, *The Presidential Character.*

6 | Evaluating the Reagan Presidency

Ronald Reagan came to the American presidency in January 1981 after his impressive 1980 presidential election victory over President Jimmy Carter. Reagan, by most accounts, won the election essentially because he was not Jimmy Carter. In 1984, Reagan won his second impressive presidential election by defeating Walter Mondale, Carter's former vice-president. This time Reagan won precisely because he was Ronald Reagan. A majority of voters clearly responded to Reagan's personal qualities and many even responded to some of Reagan's issue stands. By most accounts Reagan was viewed as a strong leader.

Reagan in his first term restored the strong presidency and lived up to the components of the macho presidential style. Reagan was strong and aggressive. He was portrayed as a winner, a competitor, and a sports fan. He was said to be decisive and competent. Moreover, he was not too emotional for the job. Reagan was tough. By 1984 he had become "Ronnie Rambo."

Reagan came to the presidency promising a return to the Eisenhower years or perhaps even the Coolidge years. He offered simple solutions to complex problems. He wanted to get government "off the backs" of the people and he wanted to deregulate industry and big business. He wanted to cut taxes and to balance the budget. He promised to fight inflation and to allow the economy to grow. He promised a return to traditional values and to put God back in his country. He wanted to cut social spending and increase defense spending. He promised to get tough with terrorists and the Soviet Union. America would not be second to the USSR in military might according to Reagan.

Reagan scored points in his first year for reinstituting the macho presidential style. He demonstrated leadership by narrowing the presidential agenda and achieving victories on budget cuts, tax cuts, and arms deals. He showed that the presidency was not imperiled or impotent but it was an office that could work once again.

Most important during his first year, he survived an assassination attempt. This stroke of luck helped his presidential image by creating super-Reagan. Presidential watchers and columnists said he was a great communicator. His early successes in his administration were compared to Franklin D. Roosevelt's first one hundred days or to Lyndon Johnson's legislative successes in his first full year as president. It was said that Reagan and his wife, Nancy Reagan, restored glamour to the White House.

In 1982, Reagan's popularity remained relatively high even though the country suffered the worst economic downturn since the Great Depression of the 1930s. Massive unemployment hurt Reagan's standing in the polls ever so slightly. Moreover, the Reagan administration began running up the largest deficits in U.S. history. By 1982, "Reaganomics" had different meanings for various groups, depending on whether one was winning under Reagan or losing. His foreign policy contained the strongest anti-Soviet rhetoric since the Kennedy administration and he embarked on the largest military buildup in American history in order to appear strong against the Soviet threat.

By 1983 Reagan was able to maintain his presidential popularity even in the face of controversies surrounding the death of U.S. marines in Lebanon and the invasion of Grenada. Representative Patricia Schroeder of Colorado dubbed Reagan the "Teflon President," because nothing seemed to stick to him.

In the 1984 election year Reagan was able to show his Teflon qualities by distancing himself from his politics. Reagan emerged again as the national leader, but his policies were not as popular as he was. The year 1984 witnessed the return of patriotism and "feeling good about America." It was the year of the Olympics, Bruce Springsteen, and, most important, it was the year of Ronald Reagan over Jimmy Carter's vice-president, Walter Mondale. By winning his second presidential election in convincing style, Reagan, the "nice guy," staked a claim for presidential greatness that many presidential watchers found appealing.

Yet somewhere beyond Ronald Reagan's smile, other questions about his style of macho presidential leadership went unasked. Why was Reagan a Teflon president? Was the media going too soft on a popular president? Were Americans tired of negative criticisms about the presidency and no longer willing to listen to criticisms or dissent? Finally, was Ronald Reagan an imperial president? These questions all needed exploring during the Reagan first term but they were not seriously considered.

In the 1970s, after Arthur Schlesinger's work on the "imperial presidency" appeared, political scientists and presidential watchers picked up the term to describe a set of behavior exhibited by presidents in the institution of the presidency. The behaviors were characterized by excessive secrecy, isolation, deception, media manipulation, unilateral war making, imperialism, and a blatant disregard for Congress and public opinion. The Ford and Carter presidencies ushered in the post-Watergate presidency, and by the end of the Carter years some called the presidency the imperiled presidency rather than the imperial.

The Reagan administration was said to have returned the presidency to the stature of the strong presidency, a presidency that could work. No one used the term "imperial presidency" as a descriptive term for the Reagan presidency in the 1980s. Why was this the case?

If one makes an examination of the Reagan administration in terms of behaviors that were characteristically used to describe the behavior of imperial presidents, Reagan scores high. Just what has been the record of the Reagan administration with respect to excessive secrecy, isolation, deception, media manipulation, unilateral war making, imperialism, and blatant disregard for Congress and public opinion? Has he exhibited any imperial behavior and if so to what degree? If he has done this, why did presidential watchers not label him as an imperial president?

A search of the record of the Reagan administration for the first term reveals that Reagan clearly took enough actions in the categories that make up the imperial presidency to be labeled as an imperial president. His administration by most accounts has been one of the most secretive and isolated administrations of the twentieth century. Reagan has engaged in masterly deception and media manipulation. His record of the "secret" war in Nicaragua qualifies him in the unilateral war-making category and his invasion of Grenada qualifies him in the imperialism category. The only component of the imperial presidency that Reagan lacks is one that shows blatant disregard for Congress and the public.

Thus, on six out of seven measures of the imperial presidency, Reagan scores relatively high. Yet because Reagan has not shown a blatant disregard for Congress and the public, because the media and others have stopped labeling presidents as "imperial," and because Reagan is a "nice guy," the Reagan administration has been able to escape some of the criticisms for actions that in the Lyndon Johnson presidency and the Richard Nixon presidency were criticized. The 1980s environment has called for a return to the strong presidency and a return to the macho presidential style. If one labels a presidential action imperial one is criticizing the new national mood and would be regarded as a "wimp."

Ronald Reagan's recent bombing of Libya added new legends to Reagan's attempt to reestablish the macho presidential style in American presidential leadership. He had Libya bombed on a Monday night during prime-time news not so much to end terrorism but to send macho messages to Qaddafi and to the American people. The bombing was more for us than for any other purpose. It was carried out during national news time, becoming our first prime-time bombing. The purpose was to show the American people that our macho president would not take any flack from a third-rate dictator. Since 1981 Reagan had elevated an obscure Arab leader to celebrity status in the world of superterrorists. Our national media provided Qaddafi with a forum and with the recognition he so desired. Reagan's rhetoric matched Qaddafi's word for word, slur for slur. Suddenly the Arab leader gained Hitlerian status in the United States as the "maddest" of the "mad men." Qaddafi called Reagan's hand with the Gulf of Sidra "Line of Death" challenge and Reagan responded with an easy military "victory." Qaddafi called for a new campaign against Americans and Reagan responded with retaliation for the Berlin disco killing of an American soldier. His response was a bombing raid on Libya. All of this was intended to be a victory for the macho style of the presidency. However, innocent citizens from both sides have died while Reagan and Qaddafi play out their games.

In this era of renewed American patriotism, jingoism, Reaganmania, Rambomania, and military buildup, it becomes necessary for a macho president to show a willingness to use force. The idea becomes "use it or lose it." Reagan has more than complied. He invaded Grenada in 1983 and lost 19 U.S. men in the invasion. It was a "victory" coming only a few days after a terrorist attack in Lebanon had killed 240 marines. Reagan has been trying to use force, terror, and the CIA to overthrow a government in Nicaragua since 1981. By all accounts he is engaged in state-sponsored terrorism when he tries to back the Contras. Yet to Reagan, there is a distinction between freedom fighters who are good and terrorists who are bad.

The bombing of Libya was to show Americans that Reagan meant business. It was to make Americans feel proud again. Those bombs were dropped to make us feel good about a humiliating defeat in Vietnam, to make us feel better about being held hostage 444 days by Iran, and to make us feel that the president was not impotent against terrorism. Ironically, Reagan, who in 1981 convinced Americans that he was the president who most wanted to fight terrorism, was the president who had lost the most American lives to terrorist attacks.

Reagan dramatically achieved results. He made America feel good again. The news media was supportive, the Congress was mostly quiet, and the vast majority of American citizens applauded the macho power play. Domestically, it showed how an American macho president can rally the citizens around the flag during a time of crisis. This was the clear objective of the bombings, because even the Reagan administration admitted the attack on Libya would not stop terrorism. It was a lashing out of sheer frustration.

The problem with the macho presidential style is that it excludes qualities of empathy, understanding, compassion, sympathy, sensitivity, caring, and nurturing from leadership qualities. Of more consequence is that by relying on the macho presidential style of leadership World War III could be provoked. So far Reagan has played the game only in Libya, Grenada, and Nicaragua.

REAGAN, NATIONAL SECURITY, AND CIVIL LIBERTIES

As an imperial president, Reagan likes to be in control. He is the quintessential "capitalist president." As Edward Greenberg has observed, "As capitalism came to require an activist, interventionist government to support, coordinate, protect, subsidize, and sustain its main economic institutions and processes, so too did this new form of government require a steady hand at the helm . . . this steady hand could only be that of the president."[1] That steady hand requires Reagan to control the masses in the name of capitalism. As Bruce Miroff has noted, American presidents are not comfortable with mass political action and movements.[2] Reagan is no exception. He likes to feel that he has an ability to control events in an uncertain world. Taken to an extreme, Reaganism could pose a threat to democracy.

Ronald Reagan has not reached the antiliberty excesses of a Nixon. Nevertheless, when compared to Ford and Carter, Reagan emerges as an excessively secret president. He made unusual efforts to weaken the Freedom of Information Act while trying to make more information classified. He attempted to require the use of lie detector tests for a broad range of federal employees. In short, Reagan embarked on new efforts to control information within his presidency. He went against the direction that Ford and Carter had provided for the open presidency.

Reagan was extremely isolated and very inaccessible to most of the media during his administration. He held fewer and fewer press conferences and he was unavailable for questioning. Reagan believed in controlled media like television and radio broadcast where he would have script control. His administration was also more deceptive than the Ford or Carter administrations. Reagan often distorted information during his few press conferences. He misspoke, gave false information, and exaggerated the situation to such an extent that White House reporters who covered the president would often joke about the misstatements. The situation reached its zenith in 1985 when Press Secretary Larry Speakes issued a statement correcting one of Reagan's misstatements that maintained President Reagan's statements do not reflect the policy of the Reagan administration.

Reagan attempted to manipulate the media more than the Ford or Carter administrations. He refused to allow the press to cover the initial stages of the Grenada invasion. His administration relied more on photo opportunities and pseudoevents than the Ford and Carter presidencies. The Reagan commercials for the 1984 election contained generic "feel good about America" themes which bordered on subliminal advertising.

Reagan unleashed the CIA secret warriors. He was involved in covert efforts to overthrow the Sandinista regime in Nicaragua from his first day on the job. Those efforts included covert funding, CIA training and advising, U.S. state-sponsored terrorism, blowing up bridges, mining harbors, and assassination manuals. Reagan unilaterally had declared a secret war on Nicaragua and he executed it. The CIA was allowed to return to business as usual under the Reagan presidency. Covert aid went to Afghanistan "freedom fighters" in efforts to fight the Soviets. In 1985 the press even unearthed CIA assassination plots against Qaddafi of Libya. The Reagan administration response was not to deny that the plots existed but to tighten CIA information security. Reagan's unilateral war making can best be seen in the invasion of Grenada in 1983. Reagan had no justification under international law to overthrow a Marxist regime on the island, yet it was the first unleashing of American military might under the new Reagan toughness. It was deemed to be the foreign policy success of his first administration.

Throughout Reagan's first term the major American media went easy on him. He was not held accountable for the costly marine deaths in Lebanon. He was allowed to escape accountability for stealing Jimmy Carter's 1980 debate briefing book before their first debates. He was not responsible for nuclear buildup, massive deficits, or secret wars; rather it was the Reagan administration and not Ronald Reagan.

Even though Reagan clearly has scored enough actions under the components of the imperial presidency, he will not be remembered as one. He will instead be evaluated as a strong president and tough leader who made the office work again. Imperial presidents do not smile and they are not nice guys like Ronald Reagan. Moreover, the media perhaps sensed that a majority of American people clearly liked the president and were tired of critics harping on the negative aspects of Reagan's presidency. Whatever the reasons, Reagan received a relatively easy ride in terms of criticisms for his presidential actions in his first term. The election results of 1984 showed the consequences. Reagan made Americans feel good again and by saying enough times that we were tougher and stronger, Reagan made Americans believe that we were tougher and stronger.

RONALD REAGAN AND THE LAUNCH SYNDROME

No other American president by his action has so revived the possibility of a nuclear confrontation with the Soviet Union than Ronald Reagan. Reagan embarked on a massive nuclear buildup from 1981 to 1985. He thought a nuclear war was winnable and he refused to negotiate with the Soviets on arms control during the first four years of his presidency. He engaged in secret testing of nuclear weapons and his administration had the Department of Defense draw up plans to fight a long nuclear war. He increased the possession of U.S. first-strike missiles such as the MX and the Trident II. Even though Reagan never actually changed the nuclear balance of power, he convinced citizens that the United States was stronger in the nuclear area than the Soviets.

Yet at the same time, he worried many other citizens. In 1984 Reagan warmed up a "dead" microphone, which turned out to be on, saying, "My fellow Americans. I am pleased to tell you I just signed legislation which outlaws Russia forever. The bombing begins in five minutes." He frightened many other citizens with the following exchange at a press conference on May 13, 1982 (*Public Papers of the President*, 1982 p. 623–24).

Question: "Mr. President, in your arms proposal, you focus on a central intercontinental missile system to the two sides. If the Soviets were to come back and say they wanted to talk about bombers, about cruise missiles, about other weapon systems, would you be willing to include those, or are those excluded?"

The President: "No, nothing is excluded. But one of the reasons for going at the ballistic missile (is that) that is the one that is the most destabilizing. That one's the one that is the most frightening to most people. And let me just give you a little reasoning . . . of my own on that score.

That is the missile sitting there in its silo in which there could be the possibility of miscalculation. That is the one that people know that once that button is pushed, there is no defense; there is no recall. And it's a matter of minutes, and the missiles reach the other country.

Those that are carried in bombers, those that are carried in ships of one kind or another, or submersibles, you are dealing there with a conventional type of weapon or instrument, and those instruments can be intercepted. They can be recalled if there has been a miscalculation. And so they don't have the same, I think, psychological effect that the presence of those other ones that, once launched, that's it; they're on their way, and there's no preventing, no stopping them."

Reagan was arguing that one could recall missiles after they had been launched.

If one is talking tough against the Soviets under a return to the macho presidential style, American citizens will accept such bravado rhetoric. Yet if a president talks haphazardly about nuclear war or jokes about World War III, citizens find the macho presidential style to be unacceptable. Macho presidents are supposed to be rational when it comes to nuclear war. This is one demand that American citizens make upon the chief executive.

American public opinion leaders like to believe that the U.S. president has the power to make the "ultimate decision," that is, whether or not to use nuclear weapons. When presidential scholars talk about the awesome burden of the American presidency, they usually mention that as "leader of the free world" the president of the United States is responsible for making the ultimate decision about the use of nuclear weapons.[3] Citizens want to believe that this so-called ultimate decision would be made by a rational president if or when the decision was made. They want their president to be of sound mind if he should be called upon to make such a decision. Citizens also want their president to be reluctant and not "trigger-happy" with respect to nuclear weapons; citizens also want assurances that nuclear weapons would be used only if it were absolutely necessary and as a last resort.

The fact that citizens, presidential watchers, and public opinion leaders want to believe that it is important to have a president who is rational, of sound mind, reluctant, and not trigger-happy with the nuclear decision can be seen in modern presidential politics with the cases of Barry Goldwater, General Curtis LeMay, Edmund Muskie, Thomas Eagleton, and Richard Nixon. In the 1964 presidential campaign, the Democratic party went to great lengths to convey the impression that Goldwater was trigger-happy. It showed a questionable commercial implying that a Goldwater presidency would mean the end of a little girl who was picking flowers because she would be destroyed in a nuclear blast. In 1968 George Wallace's running mate, General Curtis LeMay, was portrayed in some circles as a man who would abuse nuclear weapons because he talked abut the possibility of using them in a limited capacity. In 1972 Edmund Muskie was declared "unpresidential" because he broke down and cried in public over a slur against his wife during the New Hampshire primary. The *New York Times* said Muskie was "a man who tires easily and tends toward emotional outbursts under pressure."[4] The implication was that Muskie would not be a good person to make crisis decisions. Certainly he could not be trusted to make the "ultimate" decision by extension of their argument. Likewise, in the 1972 election the media attacks on the emotional and psychological fitness of Senator Thomas Eagleton centered on the fact that he would be only one heartbeat away from the presidency if he became vice-president. This kind of person then would be unacceptable as the ultimate decision maker. Finally, there was a serious outcry about Richard Nixon's emotional and psychological stability during the final days of his administration. It reached such a level that then Secretary of Defense James Schlesinger issued a memo down the military chain of command that any orders by the president for military action would also require the approval of the secretary of defense before they would be considered policy.[5]

However, even though in presidential politics we have these occasional outbursts of public reprobation against those "unstable" individuals who would dare to presume to make the ultimate decision, it really does not matter in many cases what kind of person becomes president, because the dynamics of the nuclear decision-making situation is so severely constrained that U.S. presidents can become helpless bystanders during the moments that they are supposed to be making the final decision.

Constraints

Presidential nuclear decision making during the time of the ultimate decision is severely constrained by the following:

1. a president's belief in the winnability of nuclear war
2. a president's belief in the ability to limit nuclear war
3. a president's value system that is dominated by hatred of the Soviets
4. the possibility of accidential nuclear war
5. values and beliefs of a president that can be categorized as nontrusting
6. increased technological sophistication that has outstripped presidential decision making in a nuclear decision
7. launch-on-warning systems
8. reduction of decision-making time
9. the trap that overemphasis on technology puts on a rational decision
10. the underestimation of the ability of conventional weapons to achieve a goal.

These constraints, values, beliefs, and technology have removed free, deliberate, rational choice in presidential nuclear decision making. More important, they have influenced the nuclear decision to make it more likely that the use of nuclear weapons will come about, rather than less likely. The idea that the president is rational, reluctant, and not trigger-happy is no longer relevant in a weapons delivery system that is trigger-happy itself.

The more that a U.S. president believes that a nuclear war is winnable, the more likely he is to select that course of action as a possible choice. Similarly, if a U.S. president believes that it is possible to conduct a limited, tactical nuclear war without the conflict escalating into all-out nuclear war, then the more likely that president is to use tactical weapons. Both of these beliefs encourage the use of nuclear weapons rather than discourage the use of such weapons. Moreover, beliefs that portray the "enemy" as someone who cannot be trusted, or as someone who is likely to use nuclear weapons first, constrain presidential decision making because they tilt the nuclear decision in favor of using nuclear weapons rather than mitigating against their use.

Winning Nuclear Wars

In the calculus of presidential decision making with respect to the use of nuclear weapons are two beliefs regarding the outcome of nuclear confrontation. One belief is that the United States can fight a successful limited nuclear war and win by protecting American interests. The idea is that the president would combine tactical weapons in confrontations where U.S. conventional forces could not fully protect U.S. interests. Henry Kissinger in *Nuclear Weapons and Foreign Policy* argued, "Limited nuclear war represents our most effective strategy against nuclear powers or against a major power which is capable of substituting manpower for technology."[6] For citizens, the most important part of winning a limited nuclear war would be a validation of the theory that the limited war does not spread to an all-out nuclear war. The second belief in the calculus for presidents is that an all-out nuclear war is acceptable and winnable. The assumption is that the civilian casualties are worth bearing if the enemy bears more. Thus, the decimation of civilian populations becomes the standard by which the winning of a total nuclear confrontation is judged.

With respect to the assumptions about limited nuclear war, the only American president to fight a limited and total nuclear war was Harry Truman. His decision making was not hampered by fears of escalation since the United States had a monopoly of available weapons. Even though Truman refused to kill sitting ducks as a boy, Richard Barnet has suggested that Truman more than made up for this at Hiroshima and Nagasaki.[7] As a total nuclear war, Truman was prepared to lob the entire nuclear stockpile of the United States at Japan until surrender came. This was the only time that a limited war and a total nuclear war victory were possible. Future U.S. presidents refused to use tactical nuclear weapons in Korea and Vietnam, and even Truman refused to use them again.

It is ironic that the concept of winnable nuclear war has become part of the belief system of presidential decision makers in the national security arena, because any nuclear exchange by definition is antithetical to national security. A nuclear exchange could only damage the security interests of each country involved because civilian populations, the very thing that a national security policy is supposed to protect, would be destroyed. Yet presidents still like to believe that some country could win a nuclear war. Thus the planning to "win" a nuclear exchange with the Soviet Union still goes on.

The highly publicized "doomsday exercise" by the Reagan ad-

ministration in March 1982 gave evidence that the administration
was openly practicing for nuclear war. For the first time, the Reagan administration was trying to communicate to citizens that decision makers were ready for nuclear war. The game playing also
sent a signal to the Soviet Union that the Reagan team was coor-
dinating its response in a nuclear game scenario.[8]

Richard Nixon during his final days liked to remind other decision makers that he still had the nuclear power in foreign policy.
At one meeting with loyal House Republicans during the last few
months of his tenure, Nixon told his audience, "I could pick up
that phone right now and in 25 minutes, 70 million people would
be dead."[9] Other decision makers have not been so bold when it
came to the nuclear decision. Henry Kissinger described his first
visit to inspect a Minuteman missile sight:

There is always something abstract and esoteric in the contemplation of
nuclear strategy. The visit made it more tangible and at the same time,
paradoxically more abstract. It is an awesome sight. Flying over fields of
missiles capable of destroying humanity on the basis of a single decision
by an individual of normal fallibility, whatever the safeguards, evokes a
latent uneasiness about the human condition. . . . No previous genera-
tion of statesmen has had to conduct policy in so unknown an environment
at the border line of Armageddon. . . . [The inspection] did not relieve
the unease at the fact that the survival of our civilization must be en-
trusted to a technology so out of scale with our experience and with our
capacity to grasp its limitations.[10]

Former President Jimmy Carter also realized the problems that
the nuclear threat posed to humanity. Carter wrote about this in
his memoirs when he noted, "All the glib talk about ICBM's,
MIRV's, SLCM's and GLCM's tended to lull people into indiffer-
ence or resignation about the unbelievable destruction they represented. That horror was constantly on my mind."[11]

Yet every administration since 1969 has actively planned for the
possibility of all-out nuclear war. Nixon's Executive Order 11490
detailed the responsibilities of all federal agencies following a nuclear attack. As Ed Zuckerman has shown, these government
guidelines range from the bizarre to the ludicrous.[12] For example,
the U.S. Postal Service plans to distribute emergency change-of-

address forms and the Federal Reserve system warns banks to "instruct employees on nuclear-war banking methods."[13] Presidents like to keep the myth alive that nuclear war can be planned for and that an exchange does not automatically mean the end of the United States. This planning for a "clean war" that would generate minimum civilian casualties could, as Wolfgang Panofsky has observed, "make the use of nuclear weapons in limited conflicts more acceptable."[14]

Accidental Nuclear War

The possibility of an accidental nuclear war is another constraint on rational presidential decision making with respect to the use of nuclear weapons. By accidental one means a nuclear exchange that occurs without the president having ordered a first or second strike. This idea has been within the public's consciousness at least since Stanley Kubrick's movie *Dr. Strangelove, or How I Learned to Stop Worrying and Love the Bomb*, released in February 1964.[15] As Gary Wolfe has noted about the movie,

Dr. Strangelove expands the notion of nuclear extinction—a notion obviously difficult to cope with—until we see in it all the elements of paranoia and political insanity that characterized the fifties. If we cannot deal with the notion of extinction directly, we *can* deal with the irrationality of political and military figures; we can even laugh at it. And it is this irrationality, rather than the bomb itself, which is the real focus of the film.[16]

Though most scholars within the nuclear strategy arena maintain that the movie was unrealistic and that an accidental nuclear war could not happen, others like Daniel Ellsberg are not so sure. Ellsberg believed that *Dr. Strangelove* had achieved the poetic feel of nuclear "command and control." He wrote: "When everyone was saying what an extreme parody *Dr. Strangelove* was, I remember Harry Rowan (Rand Corporation President) and I agreeing how realistic the movie was, not just in technical details, but in general atmosphere—of the military and civilian advisors."[17]

Presidential rationality in nuclear decision making would imply that presidents could rank order their preferences and select among competing alternatives to maximize their preferences. Yet as Louis Rene Beres has observed about rationality, "It does not tell us anything about whether the information used is correct or incorrect. Hence, rational actors may make errors in calculation which lead them to nuclear war and destruction."[18] Moreover, there is a tremendous amount of "operational uncertainty," as Stanley Sienkiewicz maintains, in the nuclear system.[19] Decision makers, rational and otherwise, just do not know how missiles will operate when fired, how the Soviets will respond, how the command structure will work under pressure, how the U.S. retaliation would work, or what nuclear war would be like.

The problem of the rogue commander who fires a nuclear weapon without presidential authorization still has not been totally eliminated, and perhaps it can never be. Retired Vice-Admiral Gerald Miller told a House subcommittee on internal security and scientific affairs in 1976 that the North American Air Defense Command was authorized to order a limited nuclear strike in wartime without presidential command.[20] Miller said, "Weapons he might launch would be in response to a threat of 'first use' by the opposition and under actual war conditions."[21] The problem of the isolated commander of a nuclear submarine who gets cut off from communications with the president for a certain period of time and fires a nuclear attack because he assumes the worst is a situation that continues to trouble communication experts within the command structure.

Sometimes the U.S. president could be unable to make the decision to launch because of death, disability, or removal from the communication channels. In one instance in the public record, a U.S. president was accidently separated from his operational codes needed to order an attack. Ron Nessen relates the following incident:

There was a serious security breach during a Ford visit to France in November, 1975. When Ford disembarked from Air Force One at Orly Field in Paris and boarded his motorcade, the "Football" . . . the leather briefcase containing the codes necessary to order a nuclear strike—was accidentally left behind on the plane. When the president's military aide, who was supposed to keep the briefcase close to Ford at all times, discovered it was missing, he radioed the plane and had the "Football" rushed to him in another car. But for about an hour Ford would have been unable to send the coded signal for atomic retaliation if the Russians had chosen that time for attack.[22]

Accidental war scenarios also include the problem of personnel error, mechanical failure, and computer mistakes, which could result on either side. Indeed, the whole possibility of an accidental nuclear war undercuts the rationality of presidential decision making.

SCIENCE AND ADVICE IN PRESIDENTIAL CHOICE

The importance of science, scientific advice, and new military-technological developments to the executive branch in making national security policy cannot be underestimated. During World War II a radical transformation occurred in the relationship between science and government and between scientists and the national security elite. Up until the 1940s science activity had been "pure" in the sense that as Daniel Greenberg noted, "Scientists wrote most of the rules for the use of federal research money; scientists staffed the agencies that dispensed the money, and scientists from the university community advised these same staff scientists on the distribution of money."[23]

Science activity was characterized by a peer system that encouraged pure research for knowledge's sake rather than a project system that encouraged scientists to work specifically on a project that would benefit the government. Science activity was similar to the old model of a free, laissez-faire economic system, but the experiences of World War II radically changed this system into a socialistic government-science relationship. Especially in the area of national security, science activity was no longer "pure" but was "corrupted."

Scientists entered into the new relationship as government's servant in the 1940s in a cautious manner. The executive and the national security elite controlled the political processes that determined the answers to the political questions about the use of science.[24] The experience of scientists during World War II shattered the idealistic approach that many scientists had toward their work.[25] Many scientists had been naive in thinking about the political and moral implications of the uses of their research. The work of the Manhattan Project and the atomic bombings of Hiroshima and Nagasaki destroyed the myth that science was a continuing process that would always benefit mankind.[26] As Robert Gilpin noted, "Scientists were equally as responsible for the initiation of projects which would lead to the development of new weapons as they were for the research execution of the projects."[27]

Science advice during World War II departed from the usual scientific-technical advice of the past that argued and described "what is." Science advice increasingly became more political as scientists began to argue "what should be." Some science advisors to the executive were operating under a myth that their advice was more objective, more ethically neutral and value-free than other kinds of advice. Many science advisors played upon this myth and the executive branch operated as if it believed the myth.

It is ironic that a pacifist like Albert Einstein has usually been mentioned as one of the originals who alerted Franklin Roosevelt to the possibility of atomic energy and the atomic bomb.[28] But the moving forces behind the Einstein letter to Roosevelt were Hungarian scientific émigrés Leo Szilard, Eugene Wigner, and Edward Teller who feared that Germany might be the first nation to exploit the atom for military purposes.[29] They felt that a letter from Einstein, who probably had the most respected name in science, would convince Roosevelt of the necessity for atomic research. They succeeded in their goal.

The incredible success and coordination of the Manhattan Project has been well documented.[30] Henry Stimson described it as "the greatest achievement of the combined efforts of science, industry, labor and the military in all history."[31] The success of the project also destroyed another myth about war and technology. It had generally been held by military observers that no technological innovation during a war could alter the course of that war; rather, previous wars had been won or lost due to strategy and tactics. Technological changes had occurred during other wars but they were never of the magnitude to alter the course of the war.[32] The Manhattan Project showed that scientific-military research during a war could lead to discoveries that could alter the technological advantage to one side. The actual bombings of Hiroshima and Nagasaki did not alter the course of the war, but one could see that the development of the atomic bomb could have altered the course of the war if Germany had invested more energy in the project.

Scientists contributed in many ways to the World War II effort in the United States. Scientists made advances in the "novel field of strategic bombing"[33] and contributed in the areas of submarine warfare, amphibious warfare, radar, radar jamming, rockets, proximity fuses, military medicine, and chemical-biological warfare.[34] Yet it was the success of the Manhattan Project that greatly increased the influence of secret science advice to the executive after the war.

The decision to drop the bomb has been analyzed by more scholars and students of decision making than any other war decision. The decision has been analyzed in terms of Harry Truman's involvement, the direction of strategy by a national security elite, the moral implications, and the military necessity. But one important point that usually comes out in all the studies, is that the question was never really "do we drop the bomb?" but rather "when do we drop it and where?" The lack of competing sources of alternative information and values in the decision-making process has been documented.[35] There was no great uproar within the scientific community over the use of the bomb while it was being developed. It was only after the destructive power of the bomb was revealed at Hiroshima that many scientists were morally shocked. The incredible secrecy around the Manhattan Project was responsible for stifling discussion over the morality of the bomb, which might have emerged had there been public discussion or had more members of the scientific community been aware of what was going on.

The new relationship into which science entered with the executive during World War II never subsided after the war. Especially in matters of national security policy, the relationship continued as if the war had never ended.[36] In an era of the crisis mentality for the executive, and Cold War assumptions about "monolithic communism," scientists were called upon to produce secret information for the executive. Weapons research greatly expanded. Science could no longer, as Ivan Bennett noted, "hope to exist among all human enterprises, through some mystique, without constraints or scrutiny in terms of national goals, and isolated from the competition for allocation of resources which are finite."[37] Thus the executive became the manipulator of scientific research in the name of security.[38]

Paralleling the new government-science relationship was the rise and institutionalization of the presidential secrecy system. If the new government-science relationship was said to have corrupted science, then the new secrecy system was inherently antiscience, as it smothered free and open exchanges about certain areas of scientific research. The institutionalization of the presidential secrecy system and the control of intelligence within the executive branch tremendously increased the possibility for unilateral actions by the president. Robert Oppenheimer's statement in 1950 about secrecy and national security still applies today. He precisely summed up the problem in this manner:

The decision to seek or not to seek international control of the A-bomb, the decision to try to make or not to make the H-bomb, are issues rooted in complex technical matters, that nevertheless touch the very basis of our morality. There is grave danger for us in that these decisions have been taken on the basis of facts held secret. This is not because the men who must contribute to the decisions, or must make them, are lacking in wisdom; it is because wisdom itself cannot flourish, nor even truth be determined without the give and take or debate or criticism. The relevant facts could be of little help to an enemy; yet they are indispensable for an understanding of questions of policy.[39]

Technology

Technology has altered in fundamental ways the decision-making options and posture of the American president. The use of the threat of nuclear weapons as an instrument of policy has come a long way since the Cuban Missile Crisis when, backed up by irrefutable evidence of Soviet activity in Cuba, President John Kennedy could play a nuclear card with relative safety because of the overwhelming nuclear superiority enjoyed by the United States. Technological and weapons advances in the last twenty years combined with massive Soviet nuclear arms buildup have rendered one-sided nuclear brinkmanship forever obsolete. The Cuban Missile Crisis did teach the world one profound lesson: the paradox of nuclear weapons. Nuclear weapons due to their awesome destructive power are logical only if one assumes they prevent war, because their use is unthinkable. However, if one country cannot convince its enemy that it will use nuclear weapons, then the weapons become useless as a deterrent to war.

To a great extent the technological advances with respect to nuclear weapons reflects this paradox. One tries to make the weapons larger, faster, and more sophisticated to ensure that they never need be used; at the same time one tries to increase the posturing and preparedness to convince the other side they will be used. This paradoxical behavior increases the likelihood of war and simultaneously limits presidential decision-making options. Nuclear weapons and attendant technology have seriously restricted maneuverability of decision makers because the technological advances in communications, electronics, and weapons size are offset by the fact that any nuclear use is likely to lead to all-out nuclear war with casualties beyond human comprehension. The Soviet Union has made it clear that limited nuclear war is not an option and that any nuclear war will be an all-out nuclear war.[40]

There are important strategic reasons why limited nuclear war is highly improbable if nuclear war were to erupt. The nature of the American nuclear force is a triad deployment of nuclear delivery systems consisting of fixed land-based missiles, nuclear-armed submarines, and a large strategic bomber force. Of the three legs of the triad, the submarines are virtually invulnerable to Soviet attack, but debate is intense on the vulnerability of the other two legs of the triad.[41] The United States keeps its strategic bombers on the ground, a change of policy from the 1950s and 1960s when a fully armed portion of the strategic bomber force was always airborne. Thus it is possible that a well-aimed Soviet missile attack could conceivably destroy upward of 80 percent of the U.S. land-based missile force, leaving only the sea-based force as an effective fighting unit. The United States has approximately forty nuclear-powered and nuclear-armed submarines with about sixteen usually on constant patrol. Each one is armed with sixteen missiles and each missile carries eight to ten warheads each at least four times as powerful as the Hiroshima bomb. This is clearly a potent nuclear force, and it is estimated that two submarines could destroy every major city in the Soviet Union. The submarines do have one problem, however, and that is accuracy. Since submarines are not fixed, they may have to fire missiles from points that would not ensure maximum destructive effectiveness.

If an attack were launched at U.S. missiles, it is estimated that American casualties would be from two to ten million. The president would be left with accepting these losses or escalating the war by launching the sea-based missiles at Soviet population centers. It is inconceivable that such an attack would not be followed by a second Soviet strike at American cities. The result would be an all-out nuclear war. Since both the Soviets and the Americans must assume that any launched attack against strategic missile bases would be followed by a counterattack on the other side's population centers, a first strike would have to be followed by a second strike. No other possibility is rational or logical to consider. The technology of weapons accuracy has therefore made it likely that if nuclear war were to begin, it would not be contained.

The other possibility is, of course, that an American president would accept the first-strike losses and not launch a counterattack on the Soviet Union. This would effectively amount to unconditional surrender, and it is widely believed that no American president would do this. In any event, it is deemed critical that Soviet leaders believe an American president would be willing to use nuclear weapons if sufficiently provoked. The paradox then continues; the more powerful the weapons become, the more unthinkable their use; the more unthinkable their use, the more that must be done to convince any potential adversary that they will be used.

There are several options available to deal with the problem of a strategic first strike and several involve technology. The most obvious solution to the fear of a first strike against the land-based legs to the triad is to make them invulnerable to an attack, or at least so protect them that there would be at least a 50 percent survival rate.[42] Several proposals are under consideration in the United States to increase the protection to land-based missiles and aircraft. The MX or mobile track missile system was adopted by the Carter administration but abandoned by the Reagan administration in favor of a hardening of existing missile silos. This is an acknowledged stop-gap measure until a more sophisticated technology can be developed. With respect to aircraft, the Reagan administration proposal is to develop a new large bomber, the B-1, which would replace the current strategic bomber, the B-52. The second plan which was started under the Carter administration and is continuing to be developed under the Reagan administration is the Stealth bomber, a plane that effectively would avoid detection by Soviet radar. The advantage of such an aircraft is obvious. The argument of those who believe in technological answers to basically political problems is that if our land- and air-based legs were made less vulnerable to destruction then a Soviet attack would be deterred.

Another technological option to a Soviet strategic first strike is "launch on warning." This option demands that as soon as the United States has verified a Soviet attack, the United States launches its land-based missiles against Soviet targets. The critical variable to this plan is that the U.S. missiles must be fired before the Soviet attack hits them. The ostensible advantage of launch on warning is that the sea-based missiles are held in reserve to deliver a second or even a third strike against Soviet targets. Launch on warning is made possible by advances in surveillance technology. The United States has permanent surveillance satellites over both hemispheres with the ability to detect any launching of Soviet missiles. If the Soviets were to fire missiles from land, the United States would have about a thirty-minute warning and half that time if the missiles were fired from submarines in the Atlantic or Pacific Oceans. The launch on warning is an extremely dangerous option with the very real possibility of nuclear war starting because of satellite or computer error. The technology does not really liberate the president but, in fact, limits his decision-making options without providing him with the guidance to answer the only truly critical question, "Is the attack warning an error or have the Soviets really launched?" The answer to this question is now and probably always will be a political rather than a technological one. The price of a presidential error may literally mean destruction of the civilized world. The speed at which weapons now travel eliminates the precious resource of time while our surveillance satellites provide us with the myth of warning when it comes to making the critical decision.

Technology limits presidential options in another way in that it forces one to spend money to protect what one has already acquired. This, of course, provides one with no additional security, but it does limit what a nation can spend on other military options. A prime example of this is U.S. surveillance satellites and attendant communication systems. It is hypothesized that very high altitude blasts could send out shock waves called electromagnetic pulse which can burn out transistorized and computerized communications thousands of miles away. If this were to happen during a Soviet first strike, the United States might have no effective warning of an attack and no effective means of communications to launch a counterattack. Faced with this hypothesis, the United States may find it necessary to spend large sums of money to protect surveillance satellites and communications from potential disruption. These expenditures will then further constrict presidential options.

One can understand how the evolution of technology changes the character of nuclear decision making by examining the movement from massive retaliation to mutual assured destruction (MAD) to counterforce strategy. With the technological changes that have increased the size, speed, and accuracy of nuclear weapons, the different strategies have evolved that have tended to restrict the decision options. When in the 1950s and early 1960s the United States adopted a doctrine of massive retaliation the options were fairly wide. In this period it was not likely that either nation could completely destroy the other or even effectively destroy the ability of a counterattack. This situation was altered with the introduction of the multiple independent reentry vehicle (MIRV). MIRVs carry independently targeted multiple warheads and assure that any full-scale attack would cause unacceptable casualties in this mutually assured destruction. MAD was accepted by most as a fact of life through the 1960s and 1970s, and to the extent it exists it takes nuclear decision making out of the hands of the president. Under a MAD scenario, there are no viable nuclear options because there can be no short- or long-range advantage to a first-strike nuclear attack. MAD was a policy that left the world in an apparent uneasy but stable truce. A strong argument can be made that technology had limited presidential options by insuring that nuclear war could not pay.

Technology has continued to advance, however, and so the MAD situation appears to be threatened. Technological advances have come primarily in the areas of surveillance, speed of weapons, and accuracy. Of the three, accuracy is the most important because it is now within the realm of possibility to target weapons so accurately that an enemy's land-based missile force would be destroyed. As discussed earlier this could leave one side with a possible critical advantage. This new technology has not advanced presidential options but it has created enormous pressure on both sides. With the adoption of a first-strike and counterforce option (the destruction of an enemy's land-based missiles) a new dimension of uncertainty has been added. If a crisis erupts, are the Soviets contemplating a strategic strike against U.S. land-based missiles? This consideration does not advance U.S. options because to conclude that the Soviets are about to or have just launched an attack leaves the president with only two completely unacceptable options: total capitulation or a full-scale nuclear war. There are several alternatives for dealing with the changes in nuclear policy; either one tries to overcome the uncertainties with increased technology or reduce the situation back to the uncomfortable but more stable MAD reality. Current U.S. policy appears to favor the former option though the argument seems quite strong that rather than increase security, technological advance actually further erodes national security.[43]

With respect to a nuclear strike decision, an American president has to consider three immediate criteria and a very important fourth political one. The immediate criteria concerning Soviet actions are the uncertainties of the theoretical calculations, the operational dynamics, and the psychological considerations.[44] Of the three the most critical is the psychological uncertainty a president faces concerning the Soviets. If a president were convinced the Soviets were about to attack or had actually launched an attack, regardless of the communications and surveillance data received, he would almost certainly launch an attack. Conversely, if the president were certain his Soviet counterpart would not strike first, then regardless of other factors, he would not order an attack. The reality will always, however, rest between these two extremes, leaving the president with no substantial basis on which to evaluate incoming data. Can a president actually be sure that the launch of missiles reported by surveillance satellites is not, in fact, a computer error? Technology raises the stakes and increases the data, but ultimately it does not aid in the final decision. The failure of technology to assist with the ultimate decision also operates on the fourth criterion of presidential nuclear decision making; that is, would a nuclear attack serve American ends? Would it serve, in Clausewitz's terms, the rational ends of policy?[45] Due again to uncertainties that apparently cannot be corrected, no American president can be comfortable with what will be the ultimate result of a nuclear attack. Even, for example, were the president to conclude that a first strike against Soviet missiles would result in a clear tactical victory by destroying 80 percent of the Soviet force, no U.S. president would be able to take that risk, because the cost to the United States would be too high if the president's initial calculations were incorrect.

Conclusions

Even though presidential decision making with respect to the ultimate decision is constrained by values, beliefs about the nature of nuclear war, and by technology, the macho president can still launch a first strike any time he wants to do so. The values, beliefs, and technologies that constrain macho presidents often make nuclear war a more probable rather than a less probable situation. In the name of national security these values, beliefs, and technologies lessen national security in paradoxical fashion rather than promote national security. The macho presidential style and bravado rhetoric is an appealing characteristic of Ronald Reagan's new strong presidency for some citizens, yet this same macho presidential style is completely inappropriate when dealing with nuclear exchanges with the Soviet Union as Reagan has hopefully learned in his second term.

NOTES

1. Edward Greenberg, *The American Political System: A Radical Approach*, 3d ed. (Boston: Little, Brown, 1983), pp. 236–68. For "guardian of the system" analysis, see Michael Parenti, *Democracy for the Few*, 4th ed. (New York: St. Martin's Press, 1983), pp. 261–82.

2. Bruce Miroff, "Reassessing the Modern Presidency," *Pragmatic Illusions* (New York: David McKay, 1976), pp. 271–95; Miroff, "Presidential Leverage over Social Movements: The Johnson White House and Civil Rights," *Journal of Politics*, vol. 43, no. 1 (February 1981), pp. 2–22. For an excellent people's history see Howard Zinn, *A People's History of the United States* (New York: Harper & Row, 1980). For a comprehensive

account of repression in the United States see Robert Goldstein, *Political Repression in Modern America* (New York: Schenkman Publishing, 1978).

3. For example, see Arthur Schlesinger, Jr., *The Imperial Presidency* (New York: Popular Library, 1974) p. 169.

4. "New Hampshire Primary," editorial, *New York Times*, March 9, 1972, p. 32.

5. "Capitol Chatter," *Rolling Stone*, February 26, 1976, p. 35.

6. Henry Kissinger, *Nuclear Weapons and Foreign Policy* (Garden City, N.Y.: Doubleday, 1957), p. 166.

7. Richard Barnet, *Roots of War* (Baltimore: Pelican Books, 1973), p. 17.

8. Peter McGrath, David Martin, and Eleanor Clift, "The Doomsday Exercise," *Newsweek*, April 5, 1982, p. 31. See also Louis Rene Beres, "Nuclear Strategy and World Order: The United States Imperative" (World Order Working Paper No. 23, World Order Models Project, 1982), pp. 19–20.

9. "Capitol Chatter," p. 35.

10. Henry Kissinger, *Years of Upheaval*, (Boston: Little, Brown, 1982), pp. 1194–95.

11. Jimmy Carter, *Keeping Faith: Memoirs of a President* (New York: Bantam Books, 1982), p. 212.

12. Ed Zuckerman, "How Would the U.S. Survive a Nuclear War: Don't Worry. Our People Are Working on the Problem Right Now," *Esquire*, March 1982, pp. 37–46.

13. Ibid., p. 42.

14. Wolfgang Panofsky, "The Mutual-Hostage Relationship between America and Russia," *Foreign Affairs*, vol. 52, no. 1 (October 1973), p. 111.

15. Gary K. Wolfe, "Dr. Strangelove, Red Alert, and Patterns of Paranoia in the 1950's," *Journal of Popular Film*, vol. 5, no. 2 (1976), p. 567.

16. Ibid., p. 61.

17. Jann Wenner, "Daniel Ellsberg: The Rolling Stone Interview, Part II," *Rolling Stone*, p. 34, December 6, 1973.

18. Louis Rene Beres, "Nuclear Strategy and World Order," p. 34.

19. Stanley Sienkiewicz, "Observations on the Impact of Uncertainty in Strategic Analysis," *World Politics*, vol. 32, no. 1 (October 1979), pp. 90–110.

20. UPI, "A-Strike Could Bypass President," *Indianapolis Star*, March 19, 1976, p. 1.

21. Ibid.

22. Ron Nessen, *It Sure Looks Different from the Other Side* (Chicago: Playboy Press, 1979), p. 342.

23. Daniel Greenberg, *The Politics of American Science* (New York: Penguin, 1967), p. 330.

24. See John Donovan, *The Cold Warriors: A Policy-Making Elite* (Lexington, Mass.: D. C. Heath, 1974), for a discussion of the national security elite from the 1940s to the 1970s.

25. See James Baxter, *Scientists against Time* (Boston: Little, Brown, 1946), and Lincoln Thiesmeyer and John Burchard, *Combat Scientists* (Boston: Little, Brown, 1947).

26. Robert Gilpin, *American Scientists and Nuclear Weapons Policy* (Princeton, N.J.: Princeton University Press, 1962), p. 23.

27. Ibid., p. 10.

28. See Daniel Greenberg, *The Politics of American Science*, p. 106.

29. Ibid., pp. 107–8.

30. See James Baxter, *Scientists against Time*, ch. 28, pp. 438–447.

31. Ibid., p. 438.

32. Walter Millis, *Arms and Men* (New York: Mentor Books, 1956), p. 270.

33. Bernard Brodie, *War and Politics* (New York: Macmillan, 1973), p. 458.

34. See James Baxter, *Scientists against Time*, ch. 28, p. 438.

35. See John Donovan, *The Cold Warriors*.

36. See Bruce Russett, *No Clear and Present Danger* (New York: Harper & Row, 1972), for a discussion of how the war never really ended in the minds of the national security elite. See also David Halberstam, *The Best and the Brightest* (Greenwich, Conn.: Fawcett-Crest, 1973).

37. Ivan Bennett, deputy director of the Office of Science and Technology at the time, quoted in Greenberg, *The Politics of American Science*, p. 330.

38. See Kenneth Boulding, ed., *Peace and the War Industry* (New York: Transaction, 1970), and see Henry Kissinger, ed., *Problems of National Security* (New York: Praeger, 1965).

39. Quoted in Robert Gilpin, *American Scientists and Nuclear Weapons Policy*, p. 342.

40. See Louis Rene Beres, "Nuclear Strategy and World Order," pp. 3–10.

41. Roger Morlander and Ground Zero, *Nuclear War: What's in It for You* (New York: Pocket Books, 1982), pp. 77–84.

42. James Fallows, *National Defense* (New York: Random House, 1981), pp. 144–47.

43. Morlander, *Nuclear War*, pp. 199–211.

44. Fallows, *National Defense*, pp. 148–59.

45. Beres, "Nuclear Strategy and World Order," pp. 6–7.

7 | Covering the Macho Presidential Style in the Press

Criteria for presidential greatness are largely used by scholars to grade presidents after their tenure of office is over. However, another kind of judgment is often made about presidential performance, and this judgment may affect the president's power base. This judgment is the approval or disapproval that is registered by the media during each week of the president's tenure. These judgments come in the form of *valenced* reporting.

This section looks at valenced reporting from 1900 to 1983 with respect to the American presidency in the periodical press. By valenced reporting, I mean stories that add to or subtract from the macho presidential leadership image. Stories that portray the president as winning, decisive, tough, strong, aggressive, or able to lead are considered stories that add a positive valence to the presidential image. Stories that portray the president as weak, a loser, indecisive, unable to lead, or passive are considered as negative-valenced stories which detract from the president's image.

IMAGES OF AMERICAN PRESIDENTS IN THE PERIODICAL PRESS, 1900–1983

An examination of the *Reader's Guide to Periodical Literature* gives scholars some insight into how American presidents and presidential candidates have been portrayed in the periodical press. By looking at article titles, one is in a position to look at the kinds of descriptive words that are used in making judgments about presidential performance or presidential personality by authors of periodical pieces on the presidency.

This study will trace the development of certain images by citing various articles in the periodical press which are valenced titles for the president's image.

Method

Every article *title* for every story written about the American presidents and the major presidential candidates since 1900 was coded in terms of the valence, or direction, of the article as revealed by content analysis. If the story was positive, it was scored "plus one"; if the story was neutral or if no direction in the story could be determined by the title, then a score of "zero" was given to the title of the story; and, finally, if the story was negative to the macho presidential leadership image, it received a score of "minus one."

Problems

There are many problems with this method. A story that has an obvious positive tone, such as "McKinley Wins Again," may well be a negative article once the reader gets into the body of the paper. Likewise, a story that is neutral by title during the content analysis, such as "Eisenhower Goes to Europe," might have negative reporting and analysis in the body of the article. This study used judgments based only on the title of the article to give direction as to how the periodical press was rating presidential performance.

The following data show that one can follow reporting in the *Reader's Guide to Periodical Literature* from 1900 to 1982 and measure valenced reporting with respect to American presidents and candidates.

Even though James Barber is generally given credit for focusing presidential scholars and presidential writers on the concept of "character" in the study of the presidency, in 1972, with his book *The Presidential Character*, many articles appeared at the beginning of the twentieth century that spoke about the character of the president or of a presidential candidate.[1] For example, the first presidential character article appeared on July 26, 1900, called "Personal Character of William McKinley."[2] Other character sketches appeared about William J. Bryan in 1900 and 1906, Alton Parker in 1904, Teddy Roosevelt in 1901, William Howard Taft in 1909, and Woodrow Wilson in 1912.[3]

The McKinley presidency also brought out the "good guy" story in reporting on the presidency in the twentieth century, as one story called McKinley's presidency "Good-natured Presidency" (*Nation*, March 1901). McKinley's opponent in the election of 1900 would bring out some of the first stories that portrayed presidential candidates in a highly emotional way to drive home the "radical" image of the candidate. Two article titles from 1900 make this point: "Is Bryanism Socialistic" and "Foe of Social Order." In the periodical press of the twentieth century William Bryan was one of the first to be accused of not facing the issues squarely ("Bryan's Effort to Shirk the Issue," *Harper's Weekly*, August 25, 1900) and he was the first candidate to have his moral sense questioned in "Lapses in Bryan's Ethical Sense" (*Outlook*, October 17, 1908).

Theodore Roosevelt got off to a great start in his relationship with the periodical press. He was a "lover of peace"[4] and one article explained the "Energy of Roosevelt" (*Worlds Work*, October 1901). By the end of his term in office, opinion was divided on Roosevelt's use of political power. He was called "A Force for Righteousness" (*McClure*, February 1907) by some, but others questioned "Is Mr. Roosevelt a Failure" (*Arena*, March 1908) and "Is Roosevelt Destroying Prosperity" (*Current Literature*, October 1907). Another writer commented on Roosevelt's "Lack of Dignity" and he was called "Roosevelt: The Usurper" (*Current Literature*, December 19, 1908). When Theodore Roosevelt later ran as a third-party independent candidate for the presidency in 1912, he was called "The Plotter" (*Nation*, January 25, 1912) and "The Wrecker" (*Living Age*, March 30, 1912), while others questioned "Is Mr. Roosevelt Consistent?" (*Outlook*, October 26, 1912).

William Howard Taft in early portrayals by the periodical press was a "Man of Inspired Common Sense" (*Craftsman*, February 1908) who was "Trained to Be President" (*American Monthly Review of Reviews*, June 1908). He had a "Plan of Action" (*World's*

Work, December 1909) and some commented on his abilities as "Peacemaker of the Philippines" (*Putnam's*, October 1908). Yet others saw him as the "Typical Opportunist Politician" (*Arena*, July 1908) and in his first year as president some wondered if the president had delivered on his campaign promises ("Has President Taft Made Good," *Current Literature*, September 1909).

As the Taft administration proceeded, more inspired negative titles in the periodical press began to appear. He was isolated and lonely in "Loneliness of Mr. Taft" (*Current Literature*, April 1911) and he could not deliver excitement in "President's Unexciting Message" (*Current Literature*, January 1910). Without the benefit of survey research and scientific sampling methods, it was observed that Taft's popularity was slipping in "Waning of Taft's Popularity" (*Current Literature*, April 1910) and after less than two full years in office, some writers noticed a "Collapse of the Taft Administration" (*Hampton*, October 1910). It was certainly due to the "Mistakes of Taft" (*Hearst's Magazine*, June 1912) that commentators noticed "Taft's Decline" (*American Magazine*, August 1912). This caused the central power base questioned to be asked, "Can Mr. Taft Be Saved" (*Harper's Weekly*, December 30, 1911).

The administration of Woodrow Wilson brought on the increase of valenced reporting. The periodical press began to institutionalize certain kinds of reporting patterns which would reappear throughout other administrations in the twentieth century. Wilson could give a speech and have it called "Fine and Worthy Utterance" (*R. of Rs.*, September 1912) as candidate Wilson, but once he started his tenure in office it was observed that he faced many problems in "President and His Problems" (*Outlook*, March 15, 1913).

PATTERNS OF VALENCED REPORTING

Since Wilson took office in 1913 until the 1980s, positive valenced reporting about American presidents has centered on the ideas that the president is popular, winning, handling Congress, bold, decisive, decent, all-American, and a "good guy" in the titles of stories in the periodical press. The negative valenced reporting in the periodical press as revealed by titles shows more creativity in negative reporting on the presidency. Moreover, there is a diversity to the topics for which the president, regardless of who he is, can be criticized.

Negative reporting in the periodical press covers the following kinds of criticisms:

1. the president shows an inability to perform his job in a competent manner
   a. he is unable to lead
   b. he cannot cope or govern
   c. he is indecisive
   d. he caused inflation/messed up the economy
   e. he blunders
   f. he cannot handle a crisis

2. the president is having political problems
   a. he is too isolated
   b. he is a poor politician
   c. he is too unpopular
   d. he is too rigid
   e. he is a poor handler of staff

3. the president has many sides to his personality
   a. he is schizophrenic
   b. he manipulates his image
   c. he has a "new" image
   d. he is a tragic figure

4. the president is a serious threat to democracy
   a. he is a dictator
   b. he is a warmonger
   c. he is dangerous
   d. he is a lawbreaker and a corrupt man
   e. he crushes Congress
   f. he is a liar

5. the president's tenure is over
   a. he is a failure and a defeated man
   b. his presidency is on the verge of collapse
   c. he should resign
   d. he should be impeached

6. the president is an enigma

With respect to these twenty-five categories of negative valenced article titles in the periodical press, it is important to note that all presidents since 1900 have scored articles in these negative areas. It is only when a president begins to score articles in many different categories and continues to increase his frequency of negative stories in each category that his presidency begins to crumble under the weight of negative valenced reporting.

The president shows an inability to perform his job in a competent manner

The inability to lead

It is not precisely clear in the periodical press what it means not to be able to lead. Presumably it means that one does not have enough followers, but it has come to mean more. It has become a presidential disease of the twentieth century as reported by the periodical press. For example, examine the following titles: "Marionette for President" (*Nation*, June 26, 1920), "Ineffectual Mr. Coolidge" (*New Republic*, April 15, 1925), "Doubts about Mr. Hoover's Political Leadership" (*Literary Digest*, June 14, 1930), "Failure of Leadership" (*Nation*, March 17, 1951), "Lack of Leadership in Washington" (*Vital Speeches*, June 1, 1957), "Leaders Must Lead" (*Business Week*, March 17, 1962), "New Crisis in Leadership" (*Newsweek*, July 14, 1969), "Crisis of Confidence" "Our Most Ineffectual Postwar President" (*Saturday Review*, April 29, 1978), "Carter's Leadership Problems" (*USA Today*, October 1979), and "Still Looking for a Leader" (*Time*, September 10, 1979).

Can the president cope?

Closely related to the devastating negative claims that the president is not a leader is the story that questions the president's ability to cope or handle problems. This raises doubt in the reader's mind at the beginning of the article because a question is often posed in the title of the article. See, for example, "Can Nixon Govern?" (*Newsweek*, October 28, 1968), "Worries Pile up for Ford" (*U.S. News*, September 30, 1974), "Problems Pile-up Fast for Carter" (*U.S. News*, November 22, 1976), "Can Jimmy Carter Cope?" (*Newsweek*, October 24, 1977). Obviously, if the writer of the article thought the president could cope with problems, then the writer would not have raised the question in the first place.

Indecisive presidents

Presidents are elected to make decisions and one strong attack directed at American presidents in the periodical press is that the president is indecisive. Notice the following kinds of titles: "President Harding Hesitates" (*New Republic*, December 21, 1921), "Hoover Wobbles on the Dole" (*Harper's*, June 1930), "Curse of Indecision" (*Reporter*, October 17, 1957), "Mr. Nixon Waffles" (*New Republic*, October 18, 1969), and "Carter Faces the Fuzziness Issue" (*Time*, May 31, 1976).

Inflation causer/messed up economy

If the president can be held responsible for "wanting a war," he can also be held responsible for bringing on economic problems for the citizen. He might be held responsible for a depression or for inflationary periods or for his "recession." For example, see "Mr. Roosevelt's Inflation" (*Contemporary*, August 1933), "Inflation and the Fourth Term" (*New Republic*, April 12, 1943), "Carter's Economic Doodling" (*New Leader*, September 22, 1980), and "First Carter Recession" (*New Republic*, June 10, 1978).

A man who blunders

Negative reporting in the periodical press can take the form of describing a president's mistakes. It might be a gaff, a blunder, a double blunder, an error, or a mistake. No matter what it is labeled, it is clear that the president has messed things up. See "Truman's Blunders" (*New Republic*, June 3, 1946), "Truman's Double Blunder" (*Newsweek*, September 23, 1946), "President's Gaff: Truman Swallows, Slur on Marines" (*Life*, September 18, 1950), "First Blunder" (*Time*, August 25, 1952), "McGovern as Word-Eater" (*Newsweek*, June 19, 1972), "Ridicule Problem" (*Time*, January 23, 1976), "Ford's Boo-boos" (*New Republic*, October 23, 1976), "Skier Stumbles" (*Nation*, January 15, 1977), "Back from a Blunder" (*Time*, April 26, 1976), and "Behind Carter's U.N. Fiasco" (*New York*, March 24, 1980).

President in crisis

It seems that in the periodical press, the American president is always in some sort of crisis. Crisis has become synonymous with the American presidency. Presidents are elected to act in crises. The periodical press informs its readers how well the president is handling crisis. See, for example, "Political Crisis for Mr. Truman" (*U.S. News*, June 7, 1946), "President Truman Is in Trouble" (*Newsweek*, November 12, 1945), "Candidate in Crisis" (*Time*, October 31, 1960), "Nixon in a Crisis of Leadership" (*Life*, May 15, 1970), and "President Nixon's Own Crisis Syndrome" (*Newsweek*, June 8, 1970).

The President is having political problems

Too isolated

Moreover, the president can become too isolated from the American people or the press, according to periodical writers. See, for example, "Lonely Man in the White House" (*Ladies Home Journal*, April 1914), "Isolation of the President" (*Independent*, December 6, 1915), "Growing Isolation of President Wilson" (*Current Opinion*, April 1920), "President Vanishes" (*Nation*, July 4, 1953), and "Insulation of the Presidency" (*Nation*, April 22, 1968).

Poor politician

The periodical press writers do not like poor politicians. However, it is not always clear what one has to do before one is labeled a poor politician. Winning an election is not evidence alone to show political prowess; one must also demonstrate to periodical writers that one can be a good politician while in office. If he fails at this task, and the criteria for success are never specified, the president can look for a round of articles that proclaim him to be a poor politician. See "Washington's Worst Politician" (*Saturday Evening Post*, July 24, 1948), "LBJ Isn't Really the Master Politician Everybody Thinks He Is" (*Life*, July 15, 1966), "Our Worst President?" (*Commonweal*, February 17, 1978), and "Why the Worst" (*New Republic*, August 4, 1979).

Unpopular president

The periodical press also reports the state of presidential popularity with citizens. This can be in the form of straight reporting of reliable or unreliable poll data, and it can take the form of reporting one's impression about the state of presidential popularity with various elites. Regardless of the style, the article title announcing an "unpopular" president tells the reader that many people do not like the president. For example, one should examine "President Wilson's Waning Political Power" (*Fortune*, August 29, 1914), "Decline of Mr. Kennedy" (*National Review*, August 13, 1963), "Is LBJ Slipping?" (*National Review*, October 20, 1964), "Affection Gap: Popularity" (*Time*, September 23, 1966), and "Polls: New Lows for LBJ" (*U.S. News*, April 8, 1968).

Too rigid

Presidents can also be attacked because they are not flexible enough on a particular issue. Wilson was scored for his rigidity as early as 1913 in an article "President in an Obdurate State" (*Harper's Weekly*, May 10, 1913). Other presidents would later be charged with rigidity by periodical press writers.

Poor handler of staff

Presidents can be lambasted for their poor handling of staff, cabinet, or the bureaucracy. The charge is that the president is a poor administrator or an inept judge of character of those he has chosen to work for him. For example, see "Costly Resignation: Secretary Garrison and the President" (*New Republic*, February 19, 1916), "President, Scarred by Scandal, Discards a Couple of Friends" (*Newsweek*, October 22, 1951), "Disarray in the Nixon Team" (*U.S. News*, October 13, 1969), and "How Carter's Staff Plans to Avoid Another Round of Blunders" (*U.S. News*, March 20, 1978).

The president has many sides to his personality

President as schizophrenic

Faced with all of these presidential crises, sometimes candidates and presidents begin to come apart mentally according to the press. The periodical writers like to step forward to act as the nation's psychiatrist to diagnose the mental problems. See the following: "Two Mr. Wilsons" (*New Republic*, September 9, 1916), "Are There Two Eisenhowers" (*Christian Century*, October 29, 1952), "Minds of Barry Goldwater" (*Harper's*, September 1964), "Psyching Nixon"

(*Commonweal*, January 10, 1969), and the very serious problem of "Four Jimmy Carters" (*Commonweal*, August 13, 1976).

Manipulation of image

With so many different personalities available to American presidents, it becomes important for the president or the candidate to project an image to the electorate or to the public. See the following examples of periodical press reporting on the selling of an image: "Nixon Sell" (*Nation*, August 20, 1960), "Style or Substance? First Press Conference" (*Nation*, February 4, 1961), "Kennedy Image: How It's Built" (*U.S. News*, April 9, 1962), "Selling the Product Named Hubert Humphrey" (*New York Times Magazine*, October 13, 1968), and "Selling the President, 1968" (*Life*, October 10, 1969).

The "new" image

Periodical press writers are extra careful in pointing out any new changes in images. This is a particularly disturbing charge because it means that the candidate who was projecting one constant image is trying to project a "new" image. This alerts the reader to be wary of this new media product. Notice the following: "New Hoover" (*Collier's*, July 21, 1928), "New Ike?" (*Commonweal*, January 8, 1954), "New Ike in the White House" (*Saturday Evening Post*, October 16, 1954), "Again, the New Nixon" (*Nation*, May 2, 1959), "Uphill to the Old Nixon" (*New Republic*, October 3, 1960), "New Image for Nixon" (*America*, February 3, 1968), and "Again, a New Nixon" (*Newsweek*, January 25, 1971).

Tragic figure

What with all these complexes and new images and crises, the American president then often becomes a tragic figure. His story should have been better, after all the country was certainly cheering the president on. But alas, as in good drama, the president is reduced to a tragic figure by the periodical press. See "Woodrow Wilson: A Tragedy" (*New Republic*, September 8, 1920), "Hoover's Tragedy" (*New Republic*, October 19, 1932), and "Tragedy of Eisenhower" (*New Republic*, November 3, 1952).

The president is a serious threat to democracy

President as dictator

In a democracy, and especially in one that has shown great fear of concentrated, centralized political power, one devastating criticism of presidential performance is the label of "dictator." Witness the following: "Making America Safe for Autocracy" (*Outlook*, November 6, 1918), "President's Dictatorship" (*North America*, October 1918), "Is Roosevelt a Dictator" (*Living Age*, November 1938), "Power Narcotic" (*Newsweek*, August 9, 1965), and "Mr. Truman's Police State" (*Nation*, October 25, 1947).

Warmonger

Periodical press writers like macho, tough American presidents who stand tough and strong, but sometimes a president can go too far in a military buildup or in preparation for war. Realizing that many of his readers do not really want to go to war, the periodical writer sometimes attacks the president as a lover of war. A classic in this category would be "Does Roosevelt Love Peace?" (*New Republic*, September 16, 1936).

The dangerous president or presidential candidate

The periodical press takes responsibility in its article titles to warn readers and citizens of the dire consequences of selected candidates/presidents in their leadership abilities. See, for example, "Wilson Tested, Hughes Dangerous" (*Independent*, November 6, 1916), "Hoover's Charge That Smith Is Socialistic" (*Literary Digest*, November 3, 1928), "President Roosevelt's Communistic Sympathies?" (*Catholic World*, November 1936), "Devil or Demigod?" (*Life*, November 24, 1941), "Is Franklin Roosevelt the Bryan of 1932" (*Literary Digest*, June 4, 1932), "Goldwater Threat" (*Newsweek*, July 6, 1964), "Worrying about the Wallace Impact" (*Business Week*, August 17, 1968), and "How Radical Is McGovern?" (*Newsweek*, June 19, 1972).

The lawbreaking/corrupt president

Periodical writers on the American presidency enjoy fulfilling their duty to provide the American people with information about scandals. See "President Violates the Law" (*Nation*, December 30, 1931), "Corruption and the Truman Campaign" (*New Republic*, September 24, 1951), "Machiavelli?" (*Nation*, June 8, 1970), "Lancegate: Why Carter Stuck It Out" (*New York Times Magazine*, October 16, 1977), "Tiptoeing around Goobergate" (*Business Week*, April 9, 1979), and "Billygate" (*American*, August 2–9, 1980).

The man who crushes Congress

In the never-ending game played by periodical writers about how the president is doing in terms of getting his programs passed through Congress, one often reads about the president's inability to handle Congress, as if citizens require American presidents to be able to manipulate that monster. Yet sometimes a president works his mastery too well and this brings charges that he is destroying Congress or making Congress his personal puppet. See, for example, "End of Congress" (*Nation*, March 11, 1915), and "Way LBJ Runs Congress" (*U.S. News*, April 26, 1965).

The president is a liar

The most frequent kind of negative story that appears in the periodical press is the story that suggests the president is a liar, or has a credibility problem, or is covering up the truth. These stories appeared early in the twentieth century long before Richard Nixon's presidency. Some of the classics include "Evasions by Mr. Wilson" (*New Republic*, November 13, 1915), "Mr. Hoover's Misstatements" (*Nation*, October 3, 1928), "Is President Truman an Honorable Man?" (*American Mercury*, May 1951), "Hollow Man" (*New Republic*, October 17, 1960), "Credibility Gap" (*Newsweek*, January 16, 1967), "Fooling the People" (*New Republic*, August 13, 1966), "Credibility Gap" (*New Republic*, January 14, 1967), "LBJ's Credibility Gap" (*Newsweek*, December 19, 1966), "LBJ's Credibility" (*New Republic*, January 29, 1966), "Communications Gap" (*Newsweek*, December 15, 1969), "Credibility Gulf" (*Life*, October 6, 1972), "Carter's Credibility" (*Christianity Today*, April 9, 1976), and "Jimmy Carter's Pathetic Lies" (*Harper's*, March 1976).

The president's tenure is over

President as failure/defeated man

The judgments of defeat and failure are common ways to describe American presidents in the periodical press. If as Vince Lombardi reportedly said, "Winning isn't everything. . . . It's the only thing," then failure and defeat in American presidential politics are matters for incumbent concern. See, for example, "Hoover Has Failed" (*World Tomorrow*, July 1930), "Roosevelt Strategy Fails" (*Nation*, December 25, 1935), "Is Truman Licked?" (*New Republic*, October 15, 1945), "Debasing the Presidency" (*Nation*, January 29, 1968), "Is Ford Finished?" (*National Review*, January 23, 1976), "Triple Trouble for a Beleaguered President" (*Time*, December 22, 1975), "Why Carter Fails" (*Washington Monthly*, September 1978), "Feeling Helpless" (*Newsweek*, February 26, 1979).

Collapse of the presidency

If a president is called a failure or a defeated man, the next step in criticism is to talk about the collapse of his policy or his administration. This kind of story can be seen in "Collapse of Hoover" (*Canadian Forum*, December 1932) and "Collapse of Kennedy's Grand Design" (*Saturday Evening Post*, April 16, 1963).

Please resign, Mr. President

If things are not going well for a president in terms of negative valenced reporting, some periodical writers might just suggest that the president resign. Presumably this would remove the sorry politician from the political scene and the critics could get on with their business. See, for example, "We've Been Asked When Presidents Must Quit" (*U.S. News*, February 22, 1952), "Should Mr. Eisenhower Resign?" (*Commonweal*, December 20, 1957), and "Will Carter Quit?" (*Esquire*, August 29, 1978).

If he won't quit, impeach him

Periodical writers covering the presidency have a less than subtle manner of bringing up impeachment. The use of the word in the title indicates that the writer has made a serious judgment that the actions of the president are worthy of the discussion of the ultimate removal step in American politics, "presidenticide." See "Impeachment" (*U.S. News*, April 18, 1952), "Impeachment?" (*New Republic*, April 10, 1971), "Why Impeachment" (*New Republic*, May 1, 1971), and "Impeach Nixon Now" (*Commonweal*, May 26, 1972.

The president is an enigma

The periodical press writers knowingly inform the reader that the candidate or president is dangerous; cannot lead or cope; is indecisive, rigid, isolated; is one who crushes Congress and is a poor politician and warmonger; cannot handle the economy; blunders and is not popular; is a dictator and a failure on the verge of collapse; should resign or be impeached since he is a lawbreaker, liar, and a poor handler of staff; cannot handle a crisis because he is schizophrenic; and manipulates his image to become a tragic figure.

After this remarkable piece of reporting, the periodical writers then surprisingly announce that they still do not understand or know enough about the man. He is too complex; he is an enigma. In effect, the writer tells the reader to forget all the previous stories that have been written about the president because we still do not really know the man. See the following enigma stories: "Mystery of Woodrow Wilson" (*North America*, September 1916), "Great Coolidge Mystery" (*Outlook*, February 1924), "Great Coolidge Mystery" (*Harper's*, December 1925), "Hoover, An Enigma Easily Misunderstood" (*World Work*, June 28, 1928), "Roosevelt the Enigma" (*American Magazine*, April 1944), "Great Albany Enigma" (*Saturday Evening Post*, January 22, 1944), "Enigma of Gettysburg" (*Reporter*, December 29, 1955), "Enigma of President Nixon" (Garry Wills, *Saturday Evening Post*, January 25, 1969), "Well-Planned Enigma of Jimmy Carter" (*New York Times Magazine*, June 6, 1976), "Carter So Far—A Puzzle to Many" (*U.S. News*, January 31, 1977), "Why Carter Is Still a Mystery" (*U.S. News*, October 17, 1977), and "Great Carter Mystery" (*New Republic*, April 12, 1980).

Periodical press writers act as evaluators of presidential performance. They evaluate presidential behavior in at least twenty-five categories as this section has demonstrated. They make valenced judgments all of the time about presidential competency. This sampling of periodical press opinion in the twentieth century with respect to images of American presidents has demonstrated the wide range of topics for which the president can be criticized. This criticism in the periodical press is important because it can have an impact on public perceptions of how well the president is doing in office.

COMPARING COVERAGE IN THE TWENTIETH CENTURY

The coverage of the American president has increased over the years in the American periodical press. As Table 7.1 shows, the periodical press published about eleven stories per year on President William McKinley in 1900 and in 1981 there were 577 stories published about the presidency of Ronald Reagan. Moreover, Table 7.1 indicates that the "big story" for the periodical press in terms of the amount of coverage given a president or a presidential candidate generally went to Republicans. The "big story" in the early part of the twentieth century was Theodore Roosevelt. This was especially true in 1912 when Roosevelt challenged as a third-party candidate and the periodical press wrote 181 stories on him. In 1952 as Table 7.1 shows, Dwight Eisenhower was the "big story" with 345 stories in the *Reader's Guide to Periodical Literature.* In 1969, Richard Nixon broke the 400-stories-per-year barrier with 419 and in 1977 Jimmy Carter broke the 500-stories-per-year barrier with 521 stories. In 1981 Reagan set the current record with 577 stories on Reagan in periodical literature. At this rate, within the next few years, some candidate or president will soon get over 600 stories in one year.

Generally, more stories are generated about presidential candidates and presidents during election years. Moreover, the periodical press generates stories that are decidedly biased in either a positive or a negative direction. Table 7.2 shows how Republican and Democratic candidates have fared over the years in terms of valenced reporting. The table shows the number of positive stories, the number of negative stories or (N), and the percentage of positive stories or (P) in relation to all valenced (% P/P,N) reporting. Between 1900 and 1944, Republicans clearly received a dis-

Table 7.1
Stories per Year

President	Stories per Year in Periodical Press	
W. McKinley	11.0	
T. Roosevelt	63.1	(181 stories in 1912)
W. Taft	61.2	
W. Wilson	80.0	
W. Harding	52.8	
C. Coolidge	56.3	
H. Hoover	122.2	
F. Roosevelt	109.5	
H. Truman	111.3	
D. Eisenhower	196.6	(345 stories in 1952)
J. Kennedy	200.5	
L. Johnson	285.2	
R. Nixon	384.0	(419 stories in 1969)
G. Ford	278.0	
J. Carter	467.0	(521 stories in 1977)
R. Reagan	503.0	(577 stories in 1981)

proportionate amount of favorable campaign stories in the periodical press. Surprisingly, given all the criticisms of the so-called liberal press by conservatives, Republicans continued to get positive campaign coverage from 1948 to 1980 by scoring 55.4 percent positive stories compared to 32.4 percent positive stories for Democrats. Overall, from 1900 to 1980 Republican candidates for presidency have received 56.5 percent positive stories while Democrats have received only 34.7 percent positive stories.

Table 7.3 indicates the ten best presidential campaigns in the twentieth century in terms of positive press coverage, as measured

Table 7.2
Valenced Reporting in Campaigns

Party	Time Frame	Positive	Negative	% P/P,N
Democratic	1900-1944	81	114	41.5
Republican	1900-1944	124	84	59.6
Democratic	1948-1980	187	390	32.4
Republican	1948-1980	332	267	55.4
Democratic	1900-1980	268	504	34.7
Republican	1900-1980	456	351	56.5

Table 7.3
Ten Best Presidential Campaigns (in Terms of Positive Press, 1900–1980)

Rank and Name	Year	Result	%P/P,N	%-/T	Differential (%P/P,N)-(%-/T)
1. Taft	1908	W	81.8	2.8	79.0
2. Wilson	1912	W	80.0	1.4	78.6
3. Landon	1936	L	78.2	5.3	72.9
4. Dewey	1948	L	77.7	4.9	72.8
5. Dewey	1944	L	72.2	4.6	67.6
6. Nixon	1968	W	71.7	5.8	65.9
7. Harding	1920	W	66.7	2.7	64.0
8. G. Wallace	1968	L	71.4	10.0	61.4
9. Anderson	1980	L	69.4	9.3	60.1
10. Nixon	1960	L	62.9	5.9	57.0

by valenced reporting in periodical literature. Not surprisingly, Republican candidates dominate the best presidential campaigns. The table shows the percentage of positive stories in relationship to all valenced stories, the percentage of negative stories in relation to all stories including neutral stories written about the candidate, and the differential or positive press support minus negative press support. William Taft scored the best periodical press campaign in 1908 with a differential score of 79.0. Yet Table 7.3 also reveals that positive press in periodicals such as *Time, Newsweek,* and *U.S. News,* does not necessarily mean that a candidate wins the election. For example, Landon, Dewey, and Nixon (1960) had outstanding press in relation to their Democratic opponents and still lost the election. Moreover, Table 7.3 makes it clear that the media generally are favorable to a legitimate third-party challenge as seen in the favorable press of George Wallace in 1968 and in the media campaign of John Anderson in 1980. Perhaps the periodical press writers wish to keep elections interesting and thus stress the chances of the third party. Positive reporting of these third parties has yet to pay off. The only Democratic candidate to rank in the top ten periodical press campaigns is Woodrow Wilson for his 1912 campaign, which scored a differential of 78.6.

On the other hand, Table 7.4 shows the poorest presidential campaigns in terms of reception in the periodical press. In a predictable fashion, Demcoratic candidates dominate the poorest campaigns with only Republicans Herbert Hoover and Gerald Ford showing poor campaigns in 1932 and 1976, respectively. Jimmy Carter and Franklin D. Roosevelt scored half of the ten poorest campaigns of all time. Carter scored the absolute poorest presidential campaign in the twentieth century with his 1980 campaign. Carter scored the only negative differential in the twentieth century with a -21.1 score. All other presidential campaigns, including Barry Goldwater in 1964 and George McGovern in 1972, have at least been positive in the differential. Carter as incumbent president scored 11.8 percent positive support but received 32.9 percent negative coverage. Carter's 1976 campaign was not that much better, but he did score a positive differential at 12.6. Franklin Roosevelt scored the third, fifth, and tenth poorest presidential campaigns as scored by the periodical press, but, of course, he won each of the three elections.

Table 7.4
Ten Poorest Presidential Campaigns (in Terms of Negative Press, 1900–1980)

Rank and Name	Year	Result	%P/P,N	%-/T	Differential (% P/P,N)-(% -/T)
1. Carter	1980	L	11.8	32.9	-21.1
2. Truman	1948	W	26.3	23.7	2.6
3. F. Roosevelt	1940	W	21.4	17.3	4.1
4. Bryan	1900	L	25.0	16.2	8.8
5. F. Roosevelt	1944	W	23.8	12.0	11.8
6. Carter	1976	W	27.6	15.0	12.6
7. Hoover	1932	L	35.5	19.6	15.9
8. McGovern	1972	L	34.7	15.9	18.8
9. Ford	1976	L	40.7	18.8	21.9
10. F. Roosevelt	1936	W	34.6	11.5	23.1

Table 7.5 contains valenced reporting for each presidential election since 1900 and it underscores the fact that positive press does not ensure victory if you are a Republican candidate nor does negative press for a Democratic candidate ensure defeat. Yet in the twenty-one elections since 1900, the person who has had the most favorable coverage in the periodical press has won the election fifteen times. Favorable press never hurts a candidate.

Tables 7.6 and 7.7 show the best years and the poorest years that American presidents have had in terms of valenced reporting in the periodical press. Republicans scored seven of the ten best years and Democrats scored seven of the ten poorest years for American presidents. Only Kennedy, Franklin Roosevelt, and Wilson scored in the top ten for positive reporting as Democrats, and each one did this in his first year as president. Table 7.6 shows that Teddy Roosevelt had an extraordinary year in 1906 as he scored

Table 7.5
Campaign Coverage

Year	Name	Party	Positive	Neutral	Negative	%P/P,N	% − /T
1900	McKinley	R	2	10	2	50.0	14.2
	Bryan	D	2	29	6	25.0	16.2
1904	T. Roosevelt	R	6	67	4	60.0	5.1
	Parker	D	1	27	1	50.0	3.4
1908	Taft	R	9	60	2	81.8	2.8
	Bryan	D	13	31	10	56.5	18.5
1912	Wilson	D	4	69	1	80.0	1.4
	Taft	R	6	61	4	60.0	5.6
	T. Roosevelt	I	13	146	22	37.1	12.1
1916	Wilson	D	6	52	7	46.1	10.8
	Hughes	R	12	72	7	63.1	7.7
1920	Harding	R	4	68	2	66.7	2.7
	Cox	D	1	52	2	33.3	3.6
1924	Coolidge	R	3	46	2	60.0	3.9
	Davis	D	5	38	6	45.5	12.2
1928	Hoover	R	17	102	11	60.7	8.5
	Smith	D	20	99	13	60.6	9.8
1932	F. Roosevelt	D	9	63	13	40.9	15.3
	Hoover	R	11	72	20	35.5	19.6
1936	F. Roosevelt	D	9	122	17	34.6	11.5
	Landon	R	18	71	5	78.2	5.3
1940	F. Roosevelt	D	6	99	22	21.4	17.3
	Willkie	R	23	107	16	58.9	10.9
1944	F. Roosevelt	D	5	112	16	23.8	12.0
	Dewey	R	13	91	5	72.2	4.6
1948	Truman	D	10	80	28	26.3	23.7
	Dewey	R	14	63	4	77.7	4.9
1952	Eisenhower	R	55	237	30	64.7	9.3
	Stevenson	D	11	134	20	35.5	12.1
1956	Eisenhower	R	45	224	31	59.2	10.3
	Stevenson	D	18	167	13	58.1	6.5
1960	Kennedy	D	23	144	13	63.8	7.2
	Nixon	R	17	142	10	62.9	5.9
1964	Johnson	D	33	272	29	53.2	8.6
	Goldwater	R	28	292	38	42.4	10.6
1968	Nixon	R	33	176	13	71.7	5.8
	Humphrey	D	14	114	19	42.4	12.9
	Wallace	I	25	65	10	71.4	10.0
1972	Nixon	R	50	256	51	49.5	14.3
	McGovern	D	25	222	47	34.7	15.9
1976	Carter	D	28	334	64	27.6	15.0
	Ford	R	33	173	48	40.7	18.8
1980	Reagan	R	57	357	42	57.5	9.2
	Carter	D	21	299	157	11.8	32.9
	Anderson	I	25	82	11	69.4	9.3

Table 7.6
Ten Best Years of Valenced Reporting

Rank and Name	Year	Positive (%P/P,N)	Negative (% -/T)	Differential (%P/P,N) - (% -/T)
1. T. Roosevelt	1906	83.3	3.6	79.7
2. Harding	1922	75.0	4.0	71.0
3. Eisenhower	1959	75.6	7.0	68.6
4. Kennedy	1961	70.2	5.0	65.2
5. F. Roosevelt	1933	69.6	7.1	62.5
6. Coolidge	1924	70.0	12.1	57.9
7. Taft	1909	62.5	5.6	56.9
8. Wilson	1913	60.0	7.3	52.7
9. Eisenhower	1956	62.6	10.0	52.6
10. Reagan	1981	61.7	13.5	48.2

Table 7.7
Ten Poorest Years of Valenced Reporting

Rank and Name	Year	Positive (%P/P,N)	Negative (% -/T)	Differential (%P/P,N) - (% -/T)
1. Nixon	1973	13.8	44.3	-30.5
2. Carter	1980	13.4	34.8	-21.4
3. Carter	1979	19.5	36.3	-16.8
4. Nixon	1974	23.1	38.8	-15.3
5. Wilson	1920	17.6	27.4	-9.8
6. Carter	1978	23.9	32.9	-9.0
7. Truman	1952	17.1	24.5	-7.4
8. Truman	1951	22.5	28.2	-5.7
8. F. Roosevelt	1935	12.5	18.2	-5.7
10. Coolidge	1926	14.2	17.8	-3.6

a 79.7 positive differential. Eisenhower scored two fine years with the periodical press in 1956 and 1959. Other Republicans like Harding, Coolidge, Taft, and Reagan all had top-ten years.

Table 7.7 shows presidents who scored negative differentials in the poorest valenced reporting years. As one might expect, Richard Nixon scored the poorest year of any American president in the twentieth century with his Watergate year of 1973. Nixon scored 13.8 percent positive stories and 44.3 percent negative stories for a differential score of a −30.5. It is very difficult to find positive press for Nixon during 1973.

Yet the most remarkable fact that Table 7.7 demonstrates is that the Carter administration scored three out of the ten poorest years in 1978, 1979, and 1980. Carter scored the second and third poorest years of any twentieth-century president with his 1980 negative differential of −21.4 and his 1979 negative differential of −16.8. Carter had poorer years than Richard Nixon did in the Watergate year of 1974!

Clearly the periodical press "pack" turned on Carter in 1978 and never relented. Given Carter's relatively weak press showing in the periodical press during his victorious year in 1976, it can easily be seen that the periodical press did not respond positively to James Earl Carter. Moreover, Table 7.7 also shows that Harry S. Truman scored two poor years in 1951 and 1952. Calvin Coolidge is the only Republican, other than the Watergate-plagued Nixon, to make the ten poorest showings by an American president in terms of negative reporting.

When one looks at the monthly reporting from 1945 on and when one breaks down the valenced reporting in terms of months, one gets an idea of how the pack can quickly turn in a positive or negative direction in the periodical press. Table 7.8 indicates that Dwight Eisenhower scored seven out of ten of the best months in terms of positive valenced reporting in the periodical press. Eisenhower scored four perfect months where no negative story title was written and he did this in October 1956, February 1953, November 1959, and November 1956. Only John Kennedy in January 1963 and Lyndon Johnson in April 1965 scored particularly positive months as Democrats. Richard Nixon even scored the third best month of all time with his perfect showing in March 1969, and Ronald Reagan scored a heady month in May 1981.

Table 7.8
Ten Best Months of Valenced Reporting, 1945–82

Rank and Name	Month, Year		Positive	Negative	% P/P,N
1. Eisenhower	October	1956	10	0	100.00
2. Eisenhower	February	1953	8	0	100.00
3. Eisenhower	November	1959	6	0	100.00
3. Nixon	March	1969	6	0	100.00
5. Eisenhower	November	1956	5	0	100.00
6. Eisenhower	January	1956	10	1	90.90
7. L. Johnson	April	1965	7	1	87.50
8. Reagan	May	1981	13	2	86.60
9. Eisenhower	September	1959	6	1	85.70
9. Eisenhower	September	1956	6	1	85.70
9. Kennedy	January	1963	6	1	85.70

On the other hand, Table 7.9 shows the ten poorest showings for presidents since 1945 when broken down by negative valenced reporting by months in the periodical press. Jimmy Carter scored seven out of the ten poorest months. Carter scored three months in which not one single story title in any periodical could be termed positive. These months were August 1979, September 1977, and May 1980. Moreover, Carter scored the highest outcry of negative stories in terms of absolute number in his August 1980 showing. Carter scored forty-seven negative stories against his image of a macho presidential leader in this month. This was more negative stories against Carter than Nixon received in any Watergate month! When the pack attacks, there is no place to hide.

The periodical press publishes stories in a period known as the "honeymoon," which is defined here as the first six months in office. Table 7.10 shows the rankings of all presidential honeymoons in the twentieth century in terms of the percent of positive val-

Table 7.9
Ten Poorest Months of Valenced Reporting, 1945–82

Rank and Name	Month,	Year	Positive	Negative	% P/P,N
1. Carter	August	1979	0	19	0.0
2. Carter	September	1977	0	15	0.0
3. Carter	May	1980	0	13	0.0
4. Truman	April	1948	0	9	0.0
5. Nixon	December	1973	1	27	3.5
6. Carter	August	1980	2	47	4.1
7. Carter	October	1980	1	22	4.3
8. Carter	September	1979	1	20	4.7
9. Carter	July	1979	1	18	5.2
9. Nixon	August	1973	1	18	5.2

enced stories in relation to the total valenced stories. Teddy Roosevelt had the best honeymoon of all twentieth-century presidents with 88.8 percent positive stories. Gerald Ford, with his absolute pardon of Richard Nixon in September 1974, had the shortest and the poorest honeymoon in the periodical press. Ford scored less than half support in his honeymoon period at 30.6 percent positive support and, therefore, 69.4 negative reporting. Only Jimmy Carter in 1977 scored a honeymoon period that showed more negative stories written than positive stories. As Table 7.10 reveals, Republican honeymoon periods tend to be a little better than the honeymoons for Democrats.

If the periodical press writes honeymoon stories, they also write what is termed here as "divorce"-period stories. The divorce period is for the poorest six months of reporting in terms of valenced reporting during any six-month period. Table 7.11 shows that Democrats as president have scored eight out of the ten rockiest divorce periods in relationship to be periodical press. Only Rich-

Table 7.10
Honeymoon Period Valenced Reporting (First Six Months in Office)

Rank and Name	Year	Positive	Negative	% P/P,N
1. T. Roosevelt	1901-2	8	1	88.8
2. Nixon	1969	39	9	81.2
3. Eisenhower	1953	20	5	80.0
4. Coolidge	1923-4	11	3	78.5
5. Truman	1945	13	4	76.4
6. F. Roosevelt	1933	15	6	71.4
7. Hoover	1929	10	6	62.5
8. Reagan	1981	82	50	62.1
9. Kennedy	1961	14	9	60.8
10. Wilson	1913	5	4	55.5
11. L. Johnson	1963-4	22	19	53.6
12. Harding	1921	2	2	50.0
13. Taft	1909	1	1	50.0
14. Carter	1977	31	42	42.4
15. Ford	1974-5	23	52	30.6

ard Nixon in 1973 and 1974 scored poor divorce periods as a Republican since 1945.

Table 7.11 shows that Harry Truman had the worst divorce period with the media in the periodical press in the first half of 1952. Truman received only 8.7 percent support. Surprisingly, John Kennedy was going through a traumatic divorce period with the periodical press during the last half of 1963 just before he was assassinated. Kennedy had the third poorest divorce with only 12.5 percent support. Once again, Carter leads all presidents in rough divorce periods with the periodical press beating out Richard Nixon

Table 7.11
Divorce Period Valenced Reporting, 1945–82 (Poorest Press Support in a Six-Month Period)

Rank and Name	Year	Positive	Negative	% P/P,N
1. Truman	1st half 1952	2	21	8.7
2. Nixon	2nd half 1973	19	142	11.8
3. Kennedy	2nd half 1963	2	14	12.5
4. Carter	2nd half 1980	17	109	13.4
5. L. Johnson	2nd half 1967	3	19	13.6
6. Carter	2nd half 1979	16	99	13.9
7. Truman	1st half 1948	3	16	15.8
8. Carter	2nd half 1978	17	67	20.2
9. Nixon	1st half 1974	36	129	21.8
10. L. Johnson	1st half 1968	9	26	25.7

for the most divorces. Carter scored three of the worst divorce periods in the second half of 1980, the second half of 1979, and the second half of 1978. The second half of 1978 for Carter was particularly bad for him because this should have been the period to receive his most favorable periodical press with his Camp David breakthrough stories. Yet these positive stories could not match the rash of "Can Carter Cope" stories in the periodical press. Truman, Nixon, and Johnson each scored two divorce periods in the ten poorest divorces in the periodical press.

The periodical press also likes to write congressional relations stories about American presidents. The stories deal with who is supposed to be winning and who is losing, as if congressional relations with the president were some sort of game. Table 7.12 shows the frequency of congressional relations stories since 1968. The table shows that the periodical press clearly overreported the story in 1981 of Reagan's mastery of Congress. To be sure, the Reagan successes with Congress should have been reported and indeed some of Reagan's so-called victories were newsworthy. Yet budget victories and arms deal victories are hardly the stuff of monumental victories in the history of congressional-presidential relations. The periodical press was hungry, however, for such a story. Reagan's first-year successes were reported as if he was the only American president to have won a budget fight with Congress. The periodical press wrote 155 specific stories on Ronald Reagan and Congress in 1981 with thirty-nine being clearly positive and twenty-three scored as negative titles. Reagan is the only president since 1968 to score more positive stories in relation to Congress than he scored negative stories. Before Reagan, the stories ran almost three-

Table 7.12
Congressional Relations Stories, 1968–82

Year	Name	Positive	Neutral	Negative	Total
1968	Johnson	0	3	3	6
1969	Nixon	5	15	7	27
1970	Nixon	1	16	7	24
1971	Nixon	1	12	2	15
1972	Nixon	3	3	3	9
1973	Nixon	2	17	4	23
1974	Nixon	0	2	1	3
1975	Ford	0	3	3	6
1976	Ford	1	4	3	8
1977	Carter	2	38	18	58
1978	Carter	9	27	17	53
1979	Carter	4	12	8	24
1980	Carter	0	4	0	4
1980	Reagan	4	0	2	6
1981	Reagan	39	93	23	155
1982	Reagan	8	78	27	113

to-one against the president in terms of congressional relations stories. Reagan scored almost two-to-one in favor of the president. Moreover, in Reagan's first two years in office he scored 268 stories about his relationship with Congress, which is higher than all the stories written about presidential-congressional relations since 1968.

Table 7.13 compares overall press rankings of presidents since 1900 with respect to valenced reporting in the periodical press. As

Table 7.13
Overall Press Rankings, Valenced Reporting, 1900–1982

Rank and Name	% P/P,N	% N/T	Difference (% P/P,N) minus (% N/T)
1. Harding	72.7	3.2	69.5
2. T. Roosevelt	65.1	7.1	58.0
3. McKinely	66.7	9.0	57.7
4. Eisenhower	61.5	9.7	51.8
5. Taft	53.7	8.2	45.5
6. Coolidge	53.7	10.0	43.7
7. Kennedy	53.1	10.7	42.4
8. Reagan	53.4	15.3	38.1
9. Hoover	47.6	12.6	35.0
10. Wilson	45.5	12.6	32.9
11. F. Roosevelt	37.4	14.1	23.3
12. L. Johnson	37.6	14.5	23.1
13. Ford	42.1	19.5	22.6
14. Truman	35.0	20.0	15.0
15. Nixon	35.1	23.1	12.0
16. Carter	22.3	28.0	minus 5.7

one can see from this table, Warren G. Harding received the most favorable reporting from the periodical press, and Jimmy Carter clearly received the worst overall press from the periodical writers. In fact, Carter scored an overall negative differential of −5.7 to become the only American president in the twentieth century to have generally negative periodical press. Republicans scored seven out of the first eight positions with only Democrat John Kennedy ranking in the top half in seventh place. Among Republicans, only Hoover, Ford, and Nixon scored positive support under 50 percent. Democrats, other than Kennedy, all received less than 50 percent positive support.

Carter's press was so bad over his presidency that when one breaks down Carter's periodical press in terms of valenced reporting on a monthly basis, one can see that Carter scored forty-six months in a row of negative reporting. After February 1977 Carter did not have one single month where he received more positive stories than negative stories. It is very difficult for anyone to govern in such an environment. It is doubtful that even Franklin Roosevelt, the Democratic champion of surviving negative press, could have survived such a Carterian barrage of negative reporting in the periodical press.

Table 7.14 reports on valenced reporting over time since 1900 and indicates that the so-called liberal press is not that liberal in terms of the periodical press. Both Democrats and Republicans received less than 50 percent support, so negative reporting clearly outnumbers the frequency of positive stories in the periodical press.

Table 7.14
Valenced Reporting over Time, Republicans v. Democrats, 1900–1982

Party	Positive	Negative	Total	% P/P,N
Democrats (40 yrs.)	730	1454	2184	33.4
Republicans (43 yrs.)	1086	1267	2353	46.1

Yet Republicans receive 45.9 percent support whereas Democrats receive only 33.4 percent support in the periodical press. Jimmy Carter scored 11.1 percent below the average for Democrats in percent of positive stories. Carter scored even worse than a Democrat had a right to expect.

Conclusions

Although it is not clear from this study that the periodical press was out "to get" Jimmy Carter, it is certainly clear that Carter was "got" by the periodical press.[5] Whether or not the periodical press was reporting the accurate evaluation of the Carter administration is another value question which cannot be evaluated by frequencies of positive and negative stories as revealed by the *Reader's Guide to Periodical Literature*. Perhaps the negative valenced reporting of the Carter administration was an accurate assessment of the Carter presidency. Perhaps Carter deserved a worse press than Nixon, Johnson, Harding, or Hoover because of the results or lack of results of his administration. However, I do not believe that this was the case.

The negative reporting started to go against the Carter administration by March 1977. It did not end in the periodical press and in fact it has not stopped in the periodical press. The Carter image has become one of a loser, a wimp, a weakling, an incompetent, a bumbler, a corrupt man, and one of the worst presidents of all time. I believe that this is a "rat-pack" image created by opinion leaders in the periodical press. As I read the record of the Carter administration Carter did not deserve the hostile, negative, abusive press that his administration received over a four-year period. Carter was not involved in any criminal conspiracy to obstruct justice as Richard Nixon was, and Carter was not involved in any immoral war efforts like the war in Indochina, yet his negative press was more than Johnson received for Vietnam, Nixon received for Watergate, or Hoover received for the depression. In terms of frequency of negative stories, Carter was clearly not given a fair shake by the periodical press. He received two months where positive stories outnumbered negative stories and then he received forty-six straight months where negative stories about him and his image outnumbered positive stories. According to the press, Carter did not live up to the stereotypical image of the macho presidential style.

NOTES

1. James Barber, *The Presidential Character* (Englewood Cliffs, N.J.: Prentice-Hall, 1972 and 1977).

2. C. G. Grosvenor, "Personal Character of William McKinley," *Independent*, July 26, 1900, pp. 1767–69.

3. See A. White, "Character Sketch," *McClure*, July 1900, pp. 232–37; J. Creelman, "Character Sketch," *Review of Reviews*, August 1904, pp. 163–71; L. Abbott, "Character Study," *Outlook*, September 8, 1906, pp. 66–68; "Character of Taft," *Independent*, March 4, 1909, pp. 492–94; J. Ford, "Character Sketch," *Review of Reviews*, August 1912, pp. 177–84.

4. "Roosevelt, a Lover of Peace," *Outlook*, October 12, 1901.

5. For other sources on Carter and his press relations see Jody Powell, *The Other Side of the Story* (New York: Morrow, 1984); Michael B. Grossman and Martha Kumar, *Portraying the President* (Baltimore: Johns Hopkins University Press, 1981); Robert Locander, "Carter and the Press: The First Two Years," *Presidential Studies Quarterly*, vol. 10, no. 1 (Winter 1980), pp. 106–20; Bruce Miroff, "The Media and Presidential Symbolism: The Woes of Jimmy Carter," paper delivered at the Annual Meeting of the American Political Science Association, New York, N.Y., September 3–6, 1981; and see David Paletz and Robert Entman, "Presidents, Power and the Press," *Presidential Studies Quarterly*, vol. 10, no. 3 (Summer 1980), pp. 416–26.

8 | Conclusion: The Macho Presidential Style

Rather than being remembered as the American president since 1941, who lost the fewest American soldiers in combat, Carter is remembered as a weak and passive president. Rather than being cited for being the *only* American president to ever believe that our involvement in the Vietnam War was mistaken and wrong, Carter is remembered as a "wimp." As this book has shown Carter failed to live up to the dangerous requirements of the macho presidential style and his evaluators in the press never let him forget it. One writer, John Mihalec, even called Carter the first female president of the United States. He wrote:

Jimmy Carter first presented himself to the nation as a masculine personality. Naval academy. Submariner. Nuclear Engineer. Farmer. Loner. Tough governor. But once in office, he lost no time revealing his true feminine spirit. He wouldn't twist arms. He didn't like to threaten or rebuke. He wore sweaters, and scrupulously avoided the trappings of power. He even kissed Brezhnev! And we watched how far this approach got him in the jungles of Washington and the world. So in a sense, we've already had a "woman" president: Jimmy Carter. And his feminine style of leadership nearly drove us crazy.[1]

What Mihalec failed to realize was that Carter did not provide "feminine" leadership, rather he provided a break from the traditional macho, sexist style of leadership in the form of a sex-neutral or androgynous style of leadership.

Moreover, Ronald Reagan has only provided macho rhetoric with a few secret wars and a few macho invasions. This seems to have been enough for the periodical press to sense that Reagan was a "real man" and to give him a much longer honeymoon than he deserved. The press took it very easy on Reagan because he was a "nice, sincere, likeable, virile guy." In short, he was the dangerous type of leader that the male-dominated press corps and male-dominated society had always desired.

Carl Rowan has observed that while Reagan has been portrayed as a get-tough, no-nonsense, macho president by the media, Reagan has been just as unable to handle events in an uncertain world as Jimmy Carter. Rowan noted that during Reagan's presidency there had been "well-identified Americans kidnapped from Asia to Zimbabwe, U.S. diplomats flying the flag murdered, scores of U.S. Marine 'peacekeepers' killed in Lebanon, terrorist assaults on the U.S. Capitol that led to the emplacement of grates and barricades at the White House."[2]

From 1946 through 1975 U.S. armed forces were used as a political instrument by macho presidents. According to Barry Blechman and Stephen Kaplan in their book *Force without War*, the United States used the threat of force as a political instrument 215 times during this period. They defined the political use of the armed forces as occurring when "physical actions are taken by one or more components of the uniformed military services as part of a deliberate attempt by the national authorities to influence, or to be prepared to influence, specific behavior of individuals in another nation without engaging in a continuing contest of violence."[3] By using the case studies that they use for their book, one can break down the incidents by presidential administrations to see which presidents tended to use the threat of force more than others. See Table 8.1.

The only president to use "force without war" threats less than his predecessor during his first full year in the presidency was Richard Nixon. In the first full year for presidents who came to power after destabilizing events such as assassination and resignation, the new incumbents use the threat of force more than their predecessor's average. In 1964, for example, Lyndon Johnson scored twenty-one incidents compared to Kennedy's average of 13.79, and in 1975 Gerald Ford scored seven incidents which topped Nixon's

Table 8.1
The Political Use of Armed Forces by American Presidents, 1946–75

President	Tenure (yrs.)	Incidents	Incidents per year
Harry Truman	7.0	35	5.00
Dwight Eisenhower	8.0	58	7.25
John Kennedy	2.9	40	13.79
Lyndon Johnson	5.1	48	9.41
Richard Nixon	5.6	29	5.18
Gerald Ford	1.4	8	5.71

average of 5.18. Evidently, the incumbent who comes to power by unusual circumstances wants to show the world quickly that he will not be pushed around, and, in fact, he will be more willing to push others around.

John Kennedy easily led all other presidents with the use of the armed forces for political purposes with his 13.79 average per year. Lyndon Johnson ranked second with a 9.41 average and the military man, General Dwight Eisenhower, ranked third with a 7.25 average. Gerald Ford finished fourth at 5.71 average per year and Richard Nixon ranked fifth with 5.18 incidents per year. Harry S. Truman ranked last with 5.0 incidents per year during his administration. Democratic presidents with the exception of Truman tended to throw their political weight around more than Republican presidents by using the military as an instrument of political force. Some presidents use the threat of force more than others, but all American presidents are asked to play the role of being more or less macho by threatening the use of force.

Jimmy Carter simply refused to play this dangerous game in a nuclear age. He was a man of restraint in the use of force and he was a man of peace. He sincerely believed in using all diplomatic channels and he believed in negotiations. He did not believe in secret CIA paramilitary operations. In fact, he appears to be the only American president who did not use the CIA as his personal secret army. He passionately believed in human rights and he was a compassionate person. He truly believed in measures for the disadvantaged and for minorities, even though these communities did not think he did enough for them.

It has been claimed by Carter's critics that he was a "weak" leader. Yet as Bert Rockman has shown, this critique often says more about the values of the critic than about Carter's performance.[4] A look at Carter's record of legislative achievements suggests that he pushed most of his important agenda items through the Congress in one form or another by the end of his four years. But he is remembered as the president who had the poorest relations with Congress, because of his presidential style.

Rather than being congratulated on his ability to handle details and to protect options from being decided in too rapid a fashion, Carter was criticized for his indecisiveness. When he showed emotion in office, he was criticized. When Carter warned of the energy crisis, he was being "unduly alarmist."

Carter had an extraordinary amount of hostile press coverage as was indicated earlier. In this environment, presidential watchers and raters have evidently adopted limited press criteria for presidential greatness, as Reo Christenson has observed.[5] In a *Chicago Tribune* poll in 1982 of forty-nine leading scholars, Carter was ranked as one of the ten worst presidents of all time.[6] Also in 1982, a poll of 953 historians by Professor Robert Murray showed that Carter ranked twenty-fifth out of thirty-six presidents who were rated.[7] The reasons for these low rankings, I believe, have little to do with Carter's substantive, historical performance as president and more to do with the fact that he deviated from the macho presidential style. Carter tried to be a person instead of John Wayne.

ANDROGYNOUS PRESIDENTIAL STYLE

Given the routine use of the threat of armed forces for political use, and given the fact that U.S. presidents have nuclear weapons to use to throw around their macho weight, it becomes necessary to advance some type of nonmacho presidential leadership style which would hopefully eliminate some of the disastrous consequences that a strictly macho presidential style could bring about.

Presidents should be allowed to be persons rather than forced into being men who must try to fulfill the components of the macho presidential style.

A new androgynous style of presidential leadership would maximize stereotypical "feminine" components and sex-neutral values in concert with the macho presidential values. American presidential candidates and presidents would then be called upon to demonstrate qualities such as empathy and understanding, gentleness, compassion and sympathy, sensitivity to the needs of others, and the ability to nurture. Though these qualities are often included in personality tests as feminine items, they are qualities that a whole person should be asked to demonstrate in his/her leadership style.[8]

Moreover, the new androgynous style of presidential leadership would ask presidents to demonstrate a number of sex-neutral personality characteristics such as adaptability, conscientious behavior, truthful behavior, and sincerity and reliability. By combining the sex-neutral qualities and the stereotypical feminine qualities with the macho presidential style, American presidents would then be in a position to become persons, rather than the narrow macho presidents who have controlled American politics since 1787. In order to get persons as American presidents, the electorate would have to change the type of qualities they desire in their presidents. It may take a few more macho presidential disasters before this kind of change takes place in American politics, but an antimacho backlash has been developing in some segments of the electorate against the current Reagan administration. Until American politics stops rewarding stereotypical masculine values by giving macho candidates electoral victories, and until the media stops playing up items like the "wimp factor" in the 1982 Illinois gubernatorial race, the U.S. political system will continue to be dominated by macho nonpersons.

In the 1984 presidential election Walter Mondale was portrayed by the media as being "soft," "weak," and a "wimp." He was the antithesis of the macho presidential style as provided by Ronald "Rambo" Reagan. As the Democrats tried to recover from the dramatic defeat of 1984, some party leaders tried to establish a harder edge to the party. Virginia Governor Charles Robb said, "I'm tired of hearing this party and those who represent this party described as wimps."[9] By 1985 House Democrats even began to vote like "tough" Republicans on defense issues as they gave President Reagan support on nerve gas, increased "Star Wars" spending, more Midgetman nuclear missile money, and support on giving peacetime spies the death penalty.[10] All of these Democratic responses were efforts by Democrats to reclaim the macho presidential style from Ronald Reagan. The 1988 election promised to be a contest on the macho-wimp issue and some even suggested the possibility that the presidential election could be between a former pro-football quarterback and a former pro-basketball player. The components of the macho presidential style as a way to compare presidential behavior seem alive and well in the 1980s thanks to the media analysis of Reagan's and Carter's performances. The consequences of continuing such a unidimensional leadership style in the 1980s do not bode well for U.S. democracy.

NOTES

1. John Mihalec, "Hair on the President's Chest," *Wall Street Journal*, May 11, 1984, p. 30.
2. Carl Rowan, "On 'Wimps' and 'Macho Men,' " *Bridgeport Telegram*, June 2, 1984, p. 6.
3. Barry Blechman and Stephen Kaplan, *Force without War: U.S. Armed Forces as a Political Instrument* (Washington, D.C.: Brookings Institution, 1978), p. 12.
4. Bert A. Rockman, "Carter's Troubles," *Society* (July/August 1980), p. 38.
5. Reo Christenson, "Carter and Truman: A Reappraisal of Both," *Presidential Studies Quarterly*, vol. 13, no. 2 (Spring 1983), p. 322.
6. "Rating the Presidents: The Best and the Worst," *U.S. News and World Report*, January 25, 1982, p. 29.
7. Arthur Murphy, "Evaluating the Presidents of the United States," *Presidential Studies Quarterly*, vol. 14, no. 1 (Winter 1984), p. 126.
8. Sandra L. Bem, "Beyond Androgyny," in Julia Sherman and Florence Denmark, eds., *The Psychology of Women: Future Directions in Research* (New York: Wes-Den Publishers, 1978), p. 10.
9. Tom Sherwood, "Tired of Being Wimps," *Washington Post National Weekly*, July 15, 1985, p. 15.
10. Margaret Shapiro, "John Wayne Rides Again in the House," *Washington Post National Weekly*, July 15, 1985, p. 13.

Appendix:
Valenced
Reporting

Year	Name	+	0	–	T	%P/P,N	%-/Total
1900	McKinley	2	10	2	14	50.0	14.2
1901	McKinley	2	6	0	8	100.0	0.0
1901	T. Roosevelt	7	21	1	29	87.5	3.4
1902	T. Roosevelt	3	22	2	27	60.0	7.4
1903	T. Roosevelt	1	27	2	30	33.3	6.7
1904	T. Roosevelt	7	67	4	78	63.6	5.1
1905	T. Roosevelt	5	41	2	48	71.4	4.2
1906	T. Roosevelt	10	44	2	56	83.3	3.6
1907	T. Roosevelt	10	57	6	73	62.5	8.2
1908	T. Roosevelt	7	57	10	74	41.1	13.5
1909	T. Roosevelt	6	27	3	36	66.7	8.3
1908	Taft	11	60	2	73	84.6	2.7
1909	Taft	5	45	3	53	62.5	5.6
1910	Taft	3	44	7	54	30.0	12.9
1911	Taft	3	34	6	43	33.0	13.9
1912	Taft	6	61	5	72	54.5	6.9
1913	Taft	1	8	2	11	33.3	18.2
1912	Wilson	6	69	1	76	85.7	1.3
1913	Wilson	9	67	6	82	60.0	7.3
1914	Wilson	7	52	8	67	46.6	11.9
1915	Wilson	3	35	8	46	27.2	17.4
1916	Wilson	18	111	18	147	50.0	12.2
1917	Wilson	11	36	8	55	57.8	14.5
1918	Wilson	10	51	7	68	58.8	10.3
1919	Wilson	9	90	21	120	30.0	17.5
1920	Wilson	3	34	14	51	17.6	27.4
1921	Wilson	0	8	0	8	0.0	0.0

Year	Name	+	0	-	T	%P/P,N	%-/Total
1920	Harding	6	68	2	76	75.0	2.6
1921	Harding	3	50	3	56	50.0	5.3
1922	Harding	3	21	1	25	75.0	4.0
1923	Harding	4	24	0	28	100.0	0.0
1923	Coolidge	5	46	3	54	62.5	5.5
1924	Coolidge	21	44	9	74	70.0	12.1
1925	Coolidge	2	48	5	55	28.5	9.0
1926	Coolidge	1	22	5	28	14.2	17.8
1927	Coolidge	6	47	6	59	50.0	10.1
1928	Coolidge	1	26	3	30	25.0	10.0
1929	Coolidge	0	10	0	10	0.0	0.0
1928	Hoover	21	102	11	134	65.6	8.2
1929	Hoover	11	106	9	126	55.0	7.1
1930	Hoover	16	84	18	118	47.0	15.2
1931	Hoover	11	87	15	113	42.3	13.2
1932	Hoover	11	72	24	107	31.4	22.4
1933	Hoover	0	13	0	13	0.0	0.0
1932	F. Roosevelt	10	63	14	87	41.6	16.1
1933	F. Roosevelt	23	107	10	140	69.6	7.1
1934	F. Roosevelt	21	100	14	135	60.0	10.3
1935	F. Roosevelt	3	91	21	115	12.5	18.2
1936	F. Roosevelt	13	122	19	154	40.6	12.3
1937	F. Roosevelt	7	86	25	118	21.8	21.1
1938	F. Roosevelt	6	86	21	113	22.2	18.5
1939	F. Roosevelt	5	74	13	92	27.7	14.1
1940	F. Roosevelt	8	99	24	131	25.0	18.3
1941	F. Roosevelt	6	66	11	83	35.2	13.2
1942	F. Roosevelt	8	49	6	63	57.0	9.5
1943	F. Roosevelt	4	57	14	75	22.0	18.6
1944	F. Roosevelt	11	112	17	140	39.2	12.1
1945	F. Roosevelt	0	32	0	32	0.0	0.0
1945	Truman	15	120	19	154	44.1	12.3
1946	Truman	25	96	42	163	37.3	25.7
1947	Truman	9	44	6	59	60.0	15.2
1948	Truman	14	80	30	124	31.8	11.3
1949	Truman	5	37	9	51	35.7	17.6
1950	Truman	12	62	12	86	50.0	13.9
1951	Truman	9	70	31	110	22.5	28.2
1952	Truman	6	83	29	118	17.1	24.5
1953	Truman	1	24	0	25	100.0	0.0
1952	Eisenhower	75	237	33	345	69.4	9.5
1953	Eisenhower	32	188	25	245	56.1	10.2
1954	Eisenhower	23	142	17	182	57.5	9.3
1955	Eisenhower	25	179	24	228	51.0	10.5
1956	Eisenhower	52	224	31	307	62.6	10.0
1957	Eisenhower	11	130	11	152	50.0	7.2

Year	Name	+	0	-	T	%P/P,N	%-/Total
1958	Eisenhower	10	40	9	59	52.6	15.2
1959	Eisenhower	28	90	9	127	75.6	7.0
1960	Eisenhower	16	73	13	102	55.2	12.7
1961	Eisenhower	3	17	0	20	100.0	0.0
1960	Kennedy	31	144	18	193	63.2	9.3
1961	Kennedy	26	179	11	216	70.2	5.0
1962	Kennedy	16	130	23	169	41.0	13.6
1963	Kennedy	13	90	24	127	35.1	18.8
1963	Johnson	12	68	4	84	75.0	4.7
1964	Johnson	41	272	33	346	55.0	9.5
1965	Johnson	29	221	48	298	37.6	16.1
1966	Johnson	19	211	50	280	27.5	17.8
1967	Johnson	14	147	37	198	27.4	18.6
1968	Johnson	10	166	34	210	22.7	16.2
1969	Johnson	0	9	1	10	0.0	10.0
1968	Nixon	46	176	21	243	68.6	8.6
1969	Nixon	56	321	42	419	57.1	10.0
1970	Nixon	38	224	55	317	40.8	17.3
1971	Nixon	35	207	40	282	46.6	14.2
1972	Nixon	60	256	60	376	50.0	15.9
1973	Nixon	35	238	217	490	13.8	44.3
1974	Nixon	43	182	143	368	23.1	38.8
1974	Ford	22	123	50	195	30.5	25.6
1975	Ford	41	162	31	234	56.9	13.2
1976	Ford	35	173	54	262	39.3	20.6
1977	Ford	1	2	1	4	50.0	25.0
1976	Carter	39	334	80	453	32.7	17.6
1977	Carter	41	376	104	521	28.2	19.9
1978	Carter	40	219	127	386	23.9	32.9
1979	Carter	41	255	169	465	19.5	36.3
1980	Carter	27	299	174	500	13.4	34.8
1981	Carter	0	10	0	10	0.0	0.0
1980	Reagan	98	357	65	520	60.1	12.5
1981	Reagan	126	373	78	577	61.7	13.5
1982	Reagan	41	283	88	412	31.8	21.3
1983	Reagan	74	220	95	389	43.7	24.4

Bibliography

Ackerman, Frank. *Reaganomics: Rhetoric vs. Reality.* South End Press, 1982.

Adler, Bill. *Ronnie and Nancy: A Very Special Love Story.* New York: Crown, 1985.

Allison, Graham. *Essence of Decision.* Boston: Little, Brown, 1971.

Amlund, Curtis. *New Perspectives on the Presidency.* New York: Philosophical Library, 1969.

Bailey, Thomas. *Presidential Greatness.* New York: Appleton-Century-Crofts, 1966.

————. *Presidential Saints and Sinners.* New York: Free Press, 1981.

————. *The Pugnacious Presidents.* New York: Free Press, 1980.

Barber, James. *The Presidential Character.* 2d ed. Englewood Cliffs, N.J.: Prentice-Hall, 1977.

Barger, Harold. *The Impossible Presidency.* Glenview, Ill.: Scott, Foresman, 1984.

Barilleaux, Ryan. *The President and Foreign Affairs Evaluation.* New York: Praeger, 1985.

Barnet, Richard. *Roots of War.* New York: Pelican, 1972.

Barrett, Laurence. *Gambling with History.* Garden City, New York: Doubleday, 1983.

Binkley, Wilfred. *The Man in the White House.* Westport, Conn.: Greenwood Press, 1978 reprint.

Boller, Paul. *Presidential Anecdotes.* New York: Oxford University Press, 1981.

Brownstein, Ronald, and Nina Easton. *Reagan's Ruling Class.* New York: Pantheon, 1983.

Brzezinski, Zbigniew. *Power and Principle.* New York: Farrar, Straus & Giroux, 1983.

Buchanan, Bruce. *The Presidential Experience.* Englewood Cliffs, N.J.: Prentice-Hall, 1978.

Carter, Jimmy. *Why Not the Best?* New York: Bantam Books, 1976.

————. *The Presidential Campaign, 1976.* Vol. 1. Washington, D.C.: Government Printing Office, 1978.

————. *The Presidential Campaign, 1976.* Vol. II. Washington, D.C.: Government Printing Office, 1978.

————. *Public Papers of the Presidents of the United States.* Vol. 1. Washington, D.C.: Government Printing Office, 1977.

————. *Public Papers of the Presidents.* Vol. 2. 1977.

————. *Public Papers of the Presidents.* Vol. 1. 1978.

————. *Public Papers of the Presidents.* Vol. 2. 1978.

————. *Public Papers of the Presidents.* Vol. 1. 1979.

————. *Public Papers of the Presidents.* Vol. 2. 1979.

————. *Public Papers of the Presidents.* Vol. 1. 1980–81.

————. *Public Papers of the Presidents.* Vol. 2. 1980–81.

————. *President Carter, 1978.* Washington, D.C.: Congressional Quarterly Press, 1979.

————. *President Carter, 1979.* Washington, D.C.: Congressional Quarterly Press, 1980.

————. *President Carter, 1980.* Washington, D.C.: Congressional Quarterly Press, 1981.

————. *Keeping Faith.* New York: Bantam Books, 1982.

Carter, Rosalynn. *First Lady from Plains.* Boston: Houghton Mifflin, 1984.

Commager, Henry. *The Defeat of America.* New York: Simon & Schuster, 1974.

Congressional Quarterly, Inc. *President Reagan.* Washington, D.C.: Congressional Quarterly Press, 1981.

Cornwell, Elmer, ed. *The American Presidency: Vital Center.* Chicago: Scott, Foresman, 1966.

Corwin, Edward. *The President: Office and Powers.* 5th ed. New York: New York University Press, 1984.

Cronin, Thomas. *The State of the Presidency.* 2d ed. Boston: Little, Brown, 1980.

————., ed. *Rethinking the Presidency.* Boston: Little, Brown, 1982.

Cronin, Thomas, and Sanford Greenberg, eds. *The Presidential Advisory System.* New York: Harper & Row, 1969.

Dalleck, Robert. *Ronald Reagan: The Politics of Symbolism.* Cambridge, Mass.: Harvard University Press, 1984.

Davis, Vincent, ed. *The Post Imperial Presidency*. New York: Praeger, 1980.

Denton, Robert. *The Symbolic Dimensions of the American Presidency*. Prospect Heights, Ill.: Waveland Press, 1982.

Destler, I. M. *Presidents, Bureaucrats and Foreign Policy*. Princeton, N.J.: Princeton University Press, 1972.

DiClerico, Robert. *The American President*. 2d ed. Englewood Cliffs, N.J.: Prentice-Hall, 1982.

Donovan, John. *The Cold Warriors: A Policy-Making Elite*. Lexington, Mass.: D. C. Heath, 1974.

Drell, Sidney, et al. *The Reagan Strategic Defense Initiative*. Cambridge, Mass.: Ballinger, 1985.

Drew, Elizabeth. *Portrait of an Election*. New York: Simon & Schuster, 1981.

Dugger, Ronnie. *On Reagan: The Man and His Presidency*. New York: McGraw-Hill, 1983.

Dye, Thomas. *Who's Running America? The Carter Years*. 2d ed. Englewood Cliffs, N.J.: Prentice-Hall, 1979.

————. *Who's Running America? The Reagan Years*. 3d ed. Englewood Cliffs, N.J.: Prentice-Hall, 1983.

Edwards, George. *The Public Presidency*. New York: St. Martin's Press, 1983.

Edwards, George. *Presidential Influence in Congress*. San Francisco: W. H. Freeman, 1980.

Edwards, George, and Stephen Wayne. *Presidential Leadership*. New York: St. Martin's Press, 1985.

————. *Studying the Presidency*. Knoxville: University of Tennessee Press, 1983.

Edwards, George, et al. *The Presidency and Public Policy Making*. Pittsburgh: University of Pittsburgh Press, 1985.

Erickson, Paul. *Reagan Speaks: The Making of an American Myth*. New York: New York University Press, 1985.

Fishel, Jeff. *Presidents and Promises*. Washington, D.C.: Congressional Quarterly Press, 1985.

Glad, Betty. *Jimmy Carter: In Search of the White House*. New York: Norton, 1980.

Greenstein, Fred, ed. *The Reagan Presidency: An Early Assessment*. Baltimore: Johns Hopkins University Press, 1983.

Greider, William. *The Education of David Stockman and Other Americans*. New York: Dutton, 1982.

Grossman, Michael, and Martha Kumar. *Portraying the President*. Baltimore: Johns Hopkins University Press, 1981.

Haig, Alexander. *Caveat: Realism, Reagan and Foreign Policy*. New York: Macmillan, 1984.

Halperin, Morton. *Bureaucratic Politics and Foreign Policy*. Washington, D.C.: Brookings Institution, 1974.

Hargrove, Erwin, and Michael Nelson. *Presidents, Politics, and Policy*. Baltimore: Johns Hopkins University Press, 1984.

Harmel, Robert, ed. *Presidents and Their Parties*. New York: Praeger, 1983.

Hinckley, Barbara. *Problems of the Presidency*. Glenview, Ill.: Scott, Foresman, 1985.

Hodgson, Godfrey. *All Things to All Men*. New York: Simon & Schuster, 1980.

Hoxie, Gordon, et al. *Presidency and National Security Policy*. Vol. 5. New York: Center for the Study of the Presidency, 1984.

Johnson, Haynes. *In the Absence of Power*. New York: Viking Press, 1980.

Jordan, Hamilton. *Crisis: The Last Year of the Carter Presidency*. New York. G. P. Putnam's Sons, 1982.

Kellerman, Barbara. *The Political Presidency*. New York: Oxford University Press, 1984.

Kessel, John. *Presidential Parties*. Homewood, Ill.: Dorsey Press, 1984.

Lasky, Victor. *Jimmy Carter: The Man and the Myth*. New York: Marek Publishers, 1979.

Light, Paul. *The President's Agenda*. Baltimore: Johns Hopkins University Press, 1983.

Lowi, Theodore. *The Personal President*. Ithaca, New York: Cornell University Press, 1985.

McQuaid, Kim. *Big Business and Presidential Power*. New York: Morrow, 1982.

Mollenhoff, Clark. *The President Who Failed*. New York: Macmillan, 1980.

Monroe, Kristen. *Presidential Popularity and the Economy*. New York: Praeger, 1984.

Nelson, Michael, ed. *The Presidency and the Political System*. Washington, D.C.: Congressional Quarterly Press, 1984.

Neustadt, Richard. *Presidential Power*. New York: Wiley, 1980.

Orman, John. *Presidential Secrecy and Deception*. Westport, Conn.: Greenwood Press, 1980.

Ornstein, Norman, ed. *President and Congress: Assessing Reagan's First Year*. Washington, D.C.: American Enterprise Institute, 1982.

Page, Benjamin, and Mark Petracca. *The American Presidency*. New York: McGraw-Hill, 1983.

Powell, Jody. *The Other Side of the Story*. New York: Morrow, 1984.

Pyle, Christopher, and Richard Pious. *The President, Congress and the Constitution.* New York: Free Press, 1984.

Rockman, Bert. *The Leadership Question.* New York: Praeger, 1984.

Scheer, Robert. *With Enough Shovels.* New York: Random House, 1983.

Shull, Steven. *Domestic Policy Formation.* Westport, Conn.: Greenwood Press, 1983.

Smith, Hedrick, et al. *Reagan, the Man, the President.* New York: Pergamon Press, 1981.

Sorensen, Theodore. *A Different Kind of Presidency.* New York: Harper & Row, 1984.

Talbott, Stobe. *Deadly Gambits.* New York: Knopf, 1984.

Turner, Robert. *I'll Never Lie to You: Jimmy Carter in His Words.* New York: Ballantine Books, 1976.

Vance, Cyrus. *Hard Choices.* New York: Simon & Schuster, 1983.

Vance, Cyrus, and Strobe Talbott. *The Russians and Reagan.* New York: Random House, 1984.

Watson, Richard, and Norman Thomas. *The Politics of the Presidency.* New York: Wiley, 1983.

Wayne, Steven. *The Road to the White House.* 2d ed. New York: St. Martin's Press, 1984.

White, Theodore. *America in Search of Itself.* New York: Harper & Row, 1982.

Witcover, Jules. *Marathon.* New York: Signet Books, 1978.

Wooten, James. *Dasher: The Roots and Rising of Jimmy Carter.* New York: Warner Books, 1979.

Index

ABOUT THE AUTHOR

JOHN ORMAN is Associate Professor of Politics at Fairfield University. He is the author of *The Politics of Rock Music* and *Presidential Secrecy and Deception* (Greenwood Press, 1980) and has contributed articles to *Presidential Studies Quarterly*.